Cambridge Antiquarian Society

An Index to the Reports & Abstracts of Proceedings

Including Subjects and Authors of Communications and Publications.

1840-1897

Cambridge Antiquarian Society

An Index to the Reports & Abstracts of Proceedings
Including Subjects and Authors of Communications and Publications. 1840-1897

ISBN/EAN: 9783337280635

Printed in Europe, USA, Canada, Australia, Japan

Cover: Foto ©Andreas Hilbeck / pixelio.de

More available books at **www.hansebooks.com**

Cambridge Antiquarian Society.

AN INDEX

TO THE

REPORTS & ABSTRACTS OF PROCEEDINGS;

INCLUDING

SUBJECTS AND AUTHORS

OF

COMMUNICATIONS AND PUBLICATIONS.

1840—1897

Octavo Publication

No. XXX

CAMBRIDGE:

DEIGHTON, BELL & CO.; MACMILLAN & BOWES.

1898

Price Three Shillings and Sixpence.

INDEX

Cambridge Antiquarian Society.

AN INDEX

TO THE

REPORTS & ABSTRACTS OF PROCEEDINGS;

INCLUDING

SUBJECTS AND AUTHORS

OF

COMMUNICATIONS AND PUBLICATIONS.

1840—1897

CAMBRIDGE:

DEIGHTON, BELL & CO.; MACMILLAN & BOWES.

1898

The scope of the present work is indicated by the title, and will, it is hoped, be readily understood by reference to the List of Publications which precedes it. For the general arrangement, the Treasurer, Mr R. Bowes, and the Secretary, Mr T. D. Atkinson, are responsible; Mr Bowes has also prepared the List of Publications, and has seen the whole through the Press. The Index itself has been made by Mr G. J. Gray.

December, 1898.

CONTENTS.

PUBLICATIONS OF THE SOCIETY.

PUBLICATIONS. QUARTO SERIES.

VOLUME I.

I. A CATALOGUE OF THE ORIGINAL LIBRARY OF ST CATHARINE'S HALL, 1475. Ed. by Professor G. E. CORRIE, B.D. pp. viii + 11. 1840. 1s. 6d.

II. ABBREVIATA CRONICA, 1377—1469. Ed. by J. J. SMITH, M.A. pp. viii + 22 + 1 *facsimile plate*. 1840. 2s. 6d.

III. AN ACCOUNT OF THE CONSECRATION OF ABP. PARKER. Ed. by J. GOODWIN, B.D. pp. viii + 9—27 + 1 *facsimile plate*. 1841. 3s. 6d.

IV. AN APPLICATION OF HERALDRY TO THE ILLUSTRATION OF UNIVERSITY AND COLLEGIATE ANTIQUITIES. By H. A. WOODHAM, A.B. Part I. pp. 1—73 + 1 *coloured plate and illustrations in the text*. 1841. *Out of print*.

V. AN APPLICATION OF HERALDRY, ETC. By H. A. WOODHAM, M.A. Part II. pp. 75—93 + 3 *plates* (1 *coloured*). 1842. 4s. 6d.

VI. A CATALOGUE OF THE MSS. AND SCARCE BOOKS IN THE LIBRARY OF ST JOHN'S COLLEGE. By M. COWIE, M.A. Part I. pp. vii + 1—86. 1842. *Out of print*.

VII. A DESCRIPTION OF THE SEXTRY BARN AT ELY, LATELY DEMOLISHED. By Professor R. WILLIS, M.A. pp. 8 + 4 *plates*. 1843. 3s.

VIII. A CATALOGUE OF THE MSS. AND SCARCE BOOKS IN THE LIBRARY OF ST JOHN'S COLLEGE. By M. COWIE, M.A. Part II. pp. 87—162. 1843. *Out of print*.

IX. ARCHITECTURAL NOMENCLATURE OF THE MIDDLE AGES. By Professor R. WILLIS, M.A. pp. 86 + 3 *plates*. 1844. *Out of print*.

X. ROMAN AND ROMAN-BRITISH REMAINS AT AND NEAR SHEF-
FORD. By Sir HENRY DRYDEN, Bart., M.A.
AND A CATALOGUE OF COINS FROM THE SAME PLACE. By C. W. KING,
M.A. pp. 24 + 4 *plates* (3 *coloured*). 1845. 6s. 6d.

XI. SPECIMENS OF COLLEGE PLATE. By J. J. SMITH, M.A.
pp. 18 + 13 *plates*. 1845. 15s.

XII. ROMAN-BRITISH REMAINS. ON THE MATERIALS OF TWO
SEPULCHRAL VESSELS FOUND AT WARDEN. By Professor J. S.
HENSLOW, M.A. pp. 4 + 2 *plates*. 1846. 4s.

VOLUME II.

XIII. EVANGELIA AUGUSTINI GREGORIANA. A DESCRIPTION OF
MSS. 286 AND 197 IN THE PARKER LIBRARY. By J. GOODWIN, B.D.
pp. 42 + 11 *plates* (*some coloured*). 1847. 20s.

XIV. MISCELLANEOUS COMMUNICATIONS, PART I:

I. ON PALIMPSEST SEPULCHRAL BRASSES. By A. W. FRANKS. pp.
    1—6 + 1 *folding plate*.

II. ON TWO BRITISH SHIELDS FOUND IN THE ISLE OF ELY. By
    C. W. GOODWIN, M.A. pp. 7—13 + 4 *plates*.

III. A CATALOGUE OF THE BOOKS BEQUEATHED TO C. C. COLLEGE
    BY THO. MARKAUNT IN 1439. Ed. by J. O. HALLIWELL.
    pp. 15—20.

IV. THE GENEALOGICAL HISTORY OF THE FREVILLE FAMILY. By
    A. W. FRANKS. pp. 21—29 + 3 *plates* + Pedigree. 1848.
    15s.

XV. AN HISTORICAL INQUIRY TOUCHING ST CATHARINE OF
ALEXANDRIA: TO WHICH IS ADDED A SEMI-SAXON LEGEND. By
C. HARDWICK, M.A. pp. 48 + 2 *plates**. 1849. 12s.

    * [I. From the Menologium Basilianum.
      II. Coloured figure of St Catharine traced from the wall of St Martin's
           Church, Leicester.]

PUBLICATIONS. OCTAVO SERIES.

I. THE ANGLO-SAXON LEGENDS OF ST ANDREW AND ST VERO-
NICA. Ed. by C. W. GOODWIN, M.A. pp. xi + 47. 1851. 2s. 6d.

II. FRAGMENT OF A GRÆCO-EGYPTIAN WORK UPON MAGIC.
Ed. by C. W. GOODWIN, M.A. pp. x + 57 + 1 *facsimile plate*. 1852.
3s. 6d.

III. ANCIENT CAMBRIDGESHIRE. By C. C. BABINGTON, M.A.
1853. pp. viii + 78 + 4 *plates** *and a map*. 3s. 6d. (See No. XX
for 2nd edition.)

> * [Roman Stations at Cambridge, Grantchester and Bury, and Roman
> Villa at Comberton.]

IV. A HISTORY OF WATERBEACH. By W. K. CLAY, B.D.
pp. x + 148 + 3 *plates*. 1859. 5s.

V. THE DIARY OF EDWARD RUD; TO WHICH ARE ADDED
SEVERAL LETTERS OF DR BENTLEY. Ed. by H. R. LUARD, M.A.
pp. vii + 52. 1860. 2s. 6d.

VI. A HISTORY OF LANDBEACH. By W. K. CLAY, B.D. pp.
vii + 126 + 1 *plate*. 1861. 4s. 6d.

VII. A HISTORY OF HORNINGSEY. By W. K. CLAY, B.D.
pp. xv + 60. 1865. 2s. 6d.

VIII. THE CORRESPONDENCE OF RICHARD PORSON, M.A.,
FORMERLY REGIUS PROFESSOR OF GREEK Ed. by H. R. LUARD,
M.A. pp. xiii + 143. 1867. 4s. 6d.

IX. THE HISTORY OF QUEENS' COLLEGE. Part. I. 1446—1560.
By W. G. SEARLE, M.A. pp. viii + 296. 1867. 8s.

X. HISTORICAL AND ARCHITECTURAL NOTES ON GREAT ST
MARY'S CHURCH. By S. SANDARS, M.A.
TOGETHER WITH THE ANNALS OF THE CHURCH. By CANON E.
VENABLES, M.A. pp. 98 + *folding plan and 4 illustrations in the
text*. 1869. 3s.

XI. A HISTORY OF MILTON. By the late W. K. CLAY, B.D.
pp. xii + 108. 1869. 3s.

XII. THE COINS, TOKENS, AND MEDALS OF THE TOWN, COUNTY
AND UNIVERSITY OF CAMBRIDGE. By W. G. SEARLE, M.A. pp. viii
+ 40. 1871. 2s.

XIII. THE HISTORY OF QUEENS' COLLEGE. Part II. 1560—
1662. By W. G. SEARLE, M.A. pp. 297—584. 1871. 8s.

XIV. THE HISTORY AND ANTIQUITIES OF THE PARISH OF
BOTTISHAM AND OF THE PRIORY OF ANGLESEY. By EDW. HAILSTONE,
Jun. pp. xii + 372 + 7 *plates*. 1873. 12s.

XV. AN ANNOTATED LIST OF BOOKS PRINTED ON VELLUM TO BE
FOUND IN THE UNIVERSITY AND COLLEGE LIBRARIES AT CAMBRIDGE;
WITH AN APPENDIX ON THE BIBLIOGRAPHY OF CAMBRIDGE LIBRARIES.
By S. SANDARS, M.A. pp. 80. 1878. 2s.

XVI. A SUPPLEMENT TO THE HISTORY OF THE PARISH OF BOTTISHAM AND THE PRIORY OF ANGLESEY. By EDW. HAILSTONE, Jun. pp. 35. 1878. 1s.

₊ Nos. XIV and XVI, with a title-page to the whole work, form a volume. 1873—78. 13s.

XVII. JOSSELIN'S HISTORIOLA COLLEGII CORPORIS CHRISTI ET BEATAE MARIAE CANTABRIGIAE. Edited by J. W. CLARK, M.A. pp. vi + 68 *and folding plan of rooms.* 1880. 2s.

XVIII. THE BELLS OF CAMBRIDGESHIRE. By J. J. RAVEN, D.D. pp. 192 + *folding plate and illustrations in the text.* 1881. *Out of print.*

XIX. A SUPPLEMENT TO THE 'BELLS OF CAMBRIDGESHIRE,' WITH AN INDEX TO THE WHOLE WORK. By J. J. RAVEN, D.D. pp. 193—220. 1882. *Out of print.*

₊ Nos. XVIII and XIX, with a title-page to the whole work, form a volume. 1881—82. *Out of print.*

XX. ANCIENT CAMBRIDGESHIRE. By C. C. BABINGTON, M.A., F.R.S., F.S.A. Second edition much enlarged. pp. viii + 106 + *illustrations in the text and a map.* 1883. 5s.

XXI. MEMOIR OF THE REV. CALEB PARNHAM, B.D., ST JOHN'S COLLEGE. By J. R. LUNN, B.D. Second edition, much enlarged. pp. 50. 1884. 2s.

XXII. SUGGESTIONS ADDRESSED TO KING HENRY VIII. FOR A COINAGE FOR IRELAND AND THE OTHER ISLANDS BELONGING TO ENGLAND. By NICHOLAS TYERY. Edited by G. O. WHITE-COOPER, M.A., M.B., and F. J. H. JENKINSON, M.A. pp. 51 + *Illustrations on India paper* (in text). 1886. *Out of print.*

XXIII. THE DIARY OF ALDERMAN S. NEWTON (1662—1717). Edited by J. E. FOSTER, M.A. pp. xvi + 144. 1890. 5s.

XXIV. MR ESSEX'S JOURNAL OF A TOUR THROUGH PART OF FLANDERS AND FRANCE MADE IN AUGUST 1773. Edited by W. M. FAWCETT, M.A., F.S.A. pp. xxxvi + 77 + *with portrait, silhouette front., and illustrations in the text.* 1888. 5s.

XXV. THE REGISTER OF BAPTISMS, MARRIAGES, AND BURIALS IN ST MICHAEL'S PARISH, CAMBRIDGE. Edited by J. VENN, Sc.D. pp. vii + 213. 1891. 5s.

XXVI. A SHORT CALENDAR OF THE FEET OF FINES FOR CAMBRIDGESHIRE. By WALTER RYE, F.S.A. pp. vii + 196. 1891. 5s.

XXVII. INGULF AND THE HISTORIA CROYLANDENSIS. By W. G. SEARLE, M.A. pp. viii + 216 + 1 *folding plate.* 1894. 7s. 6d.

XXVIII. On the Abbey of St Edmund at Bury. By
M. R. James, Litt.D. pp. viii + 220 + *folding plan.* 1895. 7*s.* 6*d.*

XXIX. Biographical Notes on the Librarians of Trinity
College on Sir Edward Stanhope's Foundation. By Robert
Sinker, D.D. pp. xii + 86. 1897. 3*s.* 6*d.*

REPORTS AND COMMUNICATIONS. 8vo.

Reports I—X. May 6, 1841—May 6, 1850. [Not published.]

The first four Reports contain Lists of Printed and MS. Material
relating to Cambridge, and a proposal to Index the Baker, Hare,
Cole, Bowtell, and other MS. collections.

Communications, Vol. I. 1859.

Report XI. May 26, 1851. Communications, No. I. pp.
1—36. 1851. 1*s.*

Report XII. May 17, 1852. Communications, No. II. pp.
37—50 + *plate*, Roman Vessel found at Foxton. 1852. 1*s.*

Report XIII. May 2, 1853. Communications, No. III. pp.
51—80 + *plate*, Elizabethan shoe and clog found in Corpus Christi
College. 1853. 1*s.*

Report XIV. May 22, 1854. Communications, No. IV. pp.
81—124. 1854. 1*s.*

Report XV. May 14, 1855. Communications, No. V. pp.
125—176 + 3 *Illustrations*: Episcopal Figure from Mortuary Roll of
John de Hotham, Vases from Bincombe, Dorset (2). 1855. 1*s.* 6*d.*

Report XVI. May 5, 1856. Communications, No. VI. pp.
177—240. 1856. 1*s.* 6*d.*

Report XVII. May 18, 1857. Communications, No. VII.
pp. 241—286. 1857. 1*s.* 6*d.*

Report XVIII. May 17, 1858. Communications, No. VIII.
pp. 287—342 + *plate*, Arms, Millington and Woodlarke. 1858.
1*s.* 6*d.*

Report XIX. May 23, 1859. Communications, No. IX. pp.
343—374. 1*s.* 6*d.*

Communications, Vol. II. 1864.

Report XX. May 14, 1860. Communications, No. X. pp.
1—66 + *plate*, Fibulæ found at Barrington. 1860. 2*s.*

Report XXI. May 13, 1861. Communications, No. XI. pp. 67—146. 1861. 2s.

Report XXII. May 12, 1862. Communications, No. XII. pp. 147—218. 1862. 2s.

Report XXIII. May 11, 1863. Communications, No. XIII. pp. 219—294. 1863. 2s.

Report XXIV. May 9, 1864. Communications, No. XIV. pp. 295—370 + 4 *plates*: St John's Hospital, Piscina (2), Ground Plan. 1864. 2s.

COMMUNICATIONS, VOL. III. 1879.

Report XXV. May 9, 1865. Communications, No. XV (misprinted XIV). pp. 1—60. 1865. 2s.

Report XXVI. May 14, 1866. Communications, No. XVI (misprinted XV). pp. 61—118. 1866. 2s.

Report XXXIII. May 19, 1873. With Abstract of Proceedings (including Annual Reports XXVII—XXXII). 1866—1873. Communications, No. XVII. pp. 119—294 + 8 *plates*: 1. Handwriting of Dr John Edwards. 2. Facsimile, "Image of Pity." 3—6. Fulbourn Church (4 folding). 7—8. Bronze Statuette found at Earith. 1878. 8s.

Report XXXVI. May 15, 1876, with Abstract of Proceedings (including Annual Reports XXXIV, XXXV). 1873—1876. Communications, No. XVIII. pp. 295—414 + 2 *plates*, Terra Cotta Statuettes found at Tanagra. 1879. 3s.

COMMUNICATIONS, VOL. IV. 1881.

Report XXXVII. May 28, 1877. Communications, No. XIX. pp. 3—82 (no pp. 83—84) + 5 *plates*: 1. Fresco discovered in Chesterton Church. 2. Prehistoric Peruvian Stone Implements. 3. Early Runic Calendar. 4, 5. Etruscan Bronzes. 1878. 3s.

Report XXXVIII. May 27, 1878. Communications, No. XX. pp. 85—186 + 8 *plates*: 1—3. Irish Basilica, &c. 4. Flint Implements from Helwan near Cairo. 5. Map of part of the Nile. 6. Norwegian Clog Calendar. 7, 8. Flint Implements from the Barnwell River-Gravel and Chesterton Gravel-pits. 1878. *Out of print.*

Report XXXIX. May 26, 1879. Communications, No. XXI. pp. 187—312 + 6 *plates*: 1. Leaden Vessel in Trinity College Library. 2. Powder Flask in the Collection of W. B. REDFERN, Esq. 3. Mace borne by Senior Esquire Bedell. 4. Inscriptions on the Bells of King's College. 5. Arms of de l'Isle and of Arundel, Bishops of Ely (in colour). 6. Tracery on South Wall of Landbeach Church. 1881. 4s.

Report XL. May 24, 1880. Communications, No. XXII. pp. 313—432 + 8 *plates*: 1. Carved Oak Tally Board in the Collection of W. B. REDFERN, Esq. 2. Roman Potters' Kilns found at Ashdon and at Colchester. 3, 4. Trinity Church, Cambridge: 5. Stone Figure of a Mitred Abbot discovered in Trinity Church, 1878. 6. Inscribed Vase found at Guilden Morden. 7. Plan shewing position of St John Baptist's Church, Cambridge. 8. Swords in the possession of Mr W. W. FAULDEN. 1881. *Out of print.*

COMMUNICATIONS, VOL. V. 1886.

Report XLI. May 30, 1881. Communications, No. XXIII. pp. 1—56 + 12 *plates*: 1—12. Anglo-Saxon Antiquities from Barrington. 1883. 12*s.*

Report XLII. May 22, 1882. Communications, No. XXIV. pp. 57—184 + 10 *plates*: 1—6. Palæolithic Implements from South Africa. 7—10. Minster Church, Aachen. 1884. 8*s.* 6*d.*

Report XLIII. May 7, 1883. Communications, No. XXV. pp. 185—272 + 7 *plates*: Etruscan Mirrors, &c. 1884. 7*s.* 6*d.*

Report XLIV. May 26, 1884. Communications, No. XXVI. pp. 273—378. 1886. 5*s.*

COMMUNICATIONS, VOL. VI. 1891.

Report XLV. May 18, 1885. pp. i—l. Communications, No. XXVII. pp. 1—176 + *plates* 1, 2, Inscriptions, Wilne, Masham, Jarrow, &c. 1887. 7*s.* 6*d.*

Report XLVI. May 24, 1886. li—lxxxvi. Communications, No. XXVIII. pp. 177—312 + *plates* 3, 4, Eadmer's Historia Novorum. 1888. 5*s.*

Report XLVII. May 24, 1887. pp. lxxxvii—cxxvi. Communications, No. XXIX. pp. 313—346. 1890. 3*s.*

Report XLVIII. May 21, 1888. pp. cxxvii—clii. Communications, No. XXX. pp. 347—404 + 2 *plates*: Four Gnostic Gems, Ancient Earthworks between Tyne and Solway, + *Plates*: 1—18 Four Runic Calendars. 19. Fire-place in Master's Lodge, Christ's College. [No plate 20.] 21. Tympanum, Pampisford Church. 1891. 7*s.* 6*d.*

PROCEEDINGS, VOL. VII (NEW SERIES I). 1893.

Proceedings of the Cambridge Antiquarian Society, October 29, 1888, to May 27, 1889. With Communications made to the Society, No. XXXI. pp. 1—84 + *plates*: 1, 2. Linton Church. 3. Jællinge Stone, Iceland. 4—6. Antiquities at Hauxton. 7. Choir Stalls, Brampton. 8—12. Illustrations of the Bible. 13. Blue Glazed Oenochöe. 1891. 7*s.* 6*d.*

Proceedings, October 28, 1889, to May 19, 1890, with Communications, No. XXXII. pp. 85—184 + *plates*: 14—25. House of Veysey Family in Cambridge. 26—29. Great Fen Road. 30—33. Alabaster Retables from Milton and Whittlesford. 1891. 8*s*. 6*d*.

Proceedings, October 20, 1890, to May 27, 1891. With Communications, No. XXXIII. pp. 185—324 + *plates*: 34, Bird's-eye View of Clare, 1714. 35, Cambridgeshire Ditches and Tacitus. 36—38 (in text), Horham Hall. 39—41 (39 and 40 in text), Barnwell Priory. 42, (in text) Proposed bridge St John's, 1698. 1892. 7*s*. 6*d*.

PROCEEDINGS, Vol. VIII (N. S. II). 1895.

Proceedings, 26 October, 1891, to 25 May, 1892. With Communications, No. XXXIV. pp. 1—84 + *plates*: 1. Library at Cesena (and 13 illustrations in the text of Chained Books and Cases). 2—11. Pottery, Bones, &c., Cambridge Boundary Ditches. 1893. 10*s*.

Proceedings, 31 October, 1892, to 17 May, 1893. With Communications, No. XXXV. pp. 85—252 and 2 folding tables, Eton and Winchester + Plate 12 (and 1 illustration in text) Bucket, Ancient Well at Mountsorrel. 32 illustrations in text, Armorial Ensigns of University and Colleges. 2 in text; facsimiles of 2 pages in Psalter. Figure 1 Plan shewing probable extent of Castle, 2—4 in text. 5. Plan of Castle, 1785. 6 and 7 in text. Plan, Roman House at Swaffham, in text. 4 illustrations (in text). Hall of Michael House. 1894. 7*s*. 6*d*.

Proceedings, 23 October, 1893, to 16 May, 1894. With Communications, No. XXXVI. pp. 253—410 + *plates*. 13, 14. Objects found in Ancient Ditches. 15—18. Arms of Englishmen at Padua. 19, 20. Library at Zutphen, and many illustrations in the text. 1895. 7*s*. 6*d*.

PROCEEDINGS, Vol. IX (N. S. III).

(Not indexed, being still incomplete.)

Proceedings, 22 October, 1894, to 29 May, 1895. With Communications. No. XXXVII. pp. 1—164 + *plates*: 1—3 (and 5 in text), Lincoln Cathedral Library. 4—7, The Padders' Way. 1896. 7*s*. 6*d*.

Proceedings, 21 October, 1895, to 27 May, 1896. With Communications, No. XXXVIII. pp. 165—296. 1897. 5*s*.

Proceedings, 28 October, 1896, to 26 May, 1897. With Communications, No. XXXIX. pp. 297—418. 1898. 5*s*.

OCCASIONAL PUBLICATIONS.

CATALOGUE OF COINS, ROMAN AND ENGLISH SERIES, IN THE MUSEUM OF THE CAMBRIDGE ANTIQUARIAN SOCIETY. 1847. 8vo. 2s.

INDEX TO THE BAKER MSS. By four members of the Cambridge Antiquarian Society. J. J. SMITH, C. C. BABINGTON, C. W. GOODWIN, and JOSEPH POWER. 8vo. 1848. *Out of print.*

ON THE COVER OF THE SARCOPHAGUS OF RAMESES III., NOW IN THE FITZWILLIAM MUSEUM. By SAMUEL BIRCH, LL.D. 1875. 4to.
* This paper has also been printed in the Society's *Communications*, Vol. III, No. XXXV.

CATALOGUE OF THE FIRST EXHIBITION OF THE UNIVERSITY AND COLLEGE PORTRAITS HELD IN THE FITZWILLIAM MUSEUM, May, 1884. By J. W. CLARK, M.A., President. 1884. 8vo. 1s. *Out of print.*

CATALOGUE OF THE SECOND EXHIBITION OF THE UNIVERSITY AND COLLEGE PORTRAITS HELD IN THE FITZWILLIAM MUSEUM, May, 1885. By J. W. CLARK, M.A., President. 1885. 8vo. 1s. *Out of print.*

CATALOGUE OF LOAN COLLECTION OF PLATE EXHIBITED IN THE FITZWILLIAM MUSEUM, May 8, 9, 10, 1895. By J. E. FOSTER, M.A., and T. D. ATKINSON. 8vo. 1s.

EXTRA SERIES.

LUARD MEMORIAL SERIES. I. "GRACE BOOK A," CONTAINING THE PROCTORS' ACCOUNTS AND OTHER RECORDS OF THE UNIVERSITY OF CAMBRIDGE FOR THE YEARS 1454—1488. Edited by STANLEY M. LEATHES, M.A. 8vo. pp. xliv + 276. 1897. Issued to Subscribers, 21s. (Members of the Society, 15s.)
The Series to be completed in 5 Vols.

CATALOGUE OF LOAN COLLECTION OF PLATE EXHIBITED IN THE FITZWILLIAM MUSEUM, MAY 8, 9, 10, 1895. By J. E. FOSTER, M.A., and T. D. ATKINSON. Illustrated Edition. 4to. pp. xvi + 132 + 16 photogravure plates and 15 illustrations in the text. Issued to Subscribers, 21s. Copies (limited to 35, and now out of print) on Japanese paper.

LISTS OF THE MEMBERS OF THE SOCIETY. 8vo.

May 26, 1879⎫
May 24, 1880⎪ *Out of print.*
May 30, 1881⎬
May 22, 1882⎭
May 7, 1883.
May 26, 1884.
May 18, 1885⎫ *Out of print.*
May 24, 1886⎭
May 23, 1887.

May 21, 1888.
May 27, 1889.
May 19, 1890⎫ *Out of print.*
May 17, 1893⎭
May 16, 1894.
May 29, 1895.
May 27, 1896.
May 26, 1897.
May 25, 1898.

*** With the Lists have been printed the following : The Laws, since 1880 ; List of Publications, since 1882 ; List of Societies in Union, since 1884 ; Report, since 1886 ; President's Address 1887—1893 ; Summary of Accounts, since 1894.

INDEX.

ABC as an authorised school book in the xvi. century   C. iii. 363

Aachen, Minster-Church
   C. v. 131; R. xlii. xlix

Abbreviata Chronica ab anno 1377 usque ad annum 1469, edited by J. J. Smith. (1 Facsimile.) 1840 4to Pub., No. ii.

Abergele, Seal from   R. xxxix. xvi

Abington Pigotts, Parish Registers
   C. vii. 175

   Pewter plates   R. xlvii. cxi

   Ring-dial   Pr. vii. 130

   Roman coins, &c.   R. xlv. xxxi

   Roman holding   C. vi. 309

Acland, C. L., Garlick Fair and Garlick Row. 1894   Pr. viii. 313

Antiquities of the immediate past, chiefly from Shetland. 1894
   Pr. viii. 314

Acre, Various land measures known as an   R. xlviii. cxxxiv

Actors in Dr Legge's Tragedy of Richardus Tertius   C. i. 347

Acworth, George, Letters to Archbishops Pole and Parker   C. ii. 79

Adams, J. Couch, Bronze Ring-dial. 1890   Pr. vii. 130

Africa, South, Neolithic Implements
   C. v. 67

   Palaeolithic Implements   C. v. 57

Africa, West, Copper ring money used in trade   R. xli. xxv

Aix-la-Chapelle. See *Aachen*

Alabaster fragment from Papworth Everard   R. xl. xii

   retables, Milton and Whittlesford
   Pr. vii. 106

Alderney, Roman refuse pit
   Pr. vii. 175

Alemquer, Christian Inscription
   R. xlvii. cviii

Algeria, The Medrâsen in   C. iii. 379

Allbutt, T. C., Trade in Amber in ancient times. 1893   Pr. viii. 244

Allectus, Coins   C. ii. 1, 235

Allix, C. P., Excavations at Swaffham Bulbeck. 1891   Pr. vii. 221

Almandine Garnet set in gold
   R. xxxvi. 17

Altar Cloth, Lyng Church   C. vii. 4

Altar-Slab, St Benedict's Church
   C. vii. 89

Amasis, Inscription containing the name of king   R. xlvi. lxiii

Amazon, Burial urns found near the mouth of the   C. iv. 411

Amber, Etymology of the word
   Pr. viii. 244

   Necklace from Wilbraham   R. viii. 6

   trade in ancient times   Pr. viii. 244

Amcottes, Alex., Arms granted, 1549
   R. xix. 8

America, Central, Explorations in
   R. xliv. cxviii

   Monuments   R. xliii. lxxxviii

America (*continued*)
    See *Pennsylvania. New England.*
    Utah
American Pottery. See *Pottery*
Amiens, Flint implements
         R. xxii. 6; xxiii. 8
    Cathedral, Sculpture
         R. xlviii. cxxxix
Ammonites biplex, fragment
         R. xxxiii. 10
Amphora, Earthenware, from Chester-
    ton   R. xxxiii. 7
    from Haslingfield, drawing
         R. xxxvi. 23
Ampulla. See *Bottle*
Andrew, St, Legendary adventures
         R. ix. 5
Andrew, St, and St Veronica, Anglo-
    Saxon legends, edited by C. W.
    Goodwin. 1851   8vo Pub., No. i.
Andro-sphinx from Canosa
         R. xxxvi. 22
Anglesey Abbey, Grain rubber
         R. xxi. 8
Anglesey Priory, History and Anti-
    quities, by E. Hailstone. 1873–8
         8vo Pub., Nos. xiv., xvi.
Anglo-Saxon Cemetery at Barrington
         C. v. 5; R. xli. xii
    Cemetery at Girton
         R. xli. xx; xlii. li
Anglo-Saxon legend of St Veronica
         C. i. 3
    legends of St Andrew and St Ve-
    ronica   8vo Pub., No. i.
    notices of St George   R. x. 10
    remains from Barrington   C. ii. 7
    remains from Girton   R. xlvi. lxxiv
    remains from cemetery at back of
    St John's Coll.   R. xlviii. cxl
    See also *Beads. Fibula. Weapons*
Anstey, John, Brass of, at Quy
         R. xvi. 10; Woodcut, C. i. 219
Anstey's chantry at Stow-cum-Quy,
    Deed etc.   R. xvi. 10; C. i. 201
Anstey, Herts. Vase containing blood
         R. xxxviii. xviii

Anthony, John, Two steel caskets of
    xv. century from Nuremberg. 1848
         R. viii. 6
Antiquities found in digging the foun-
    dations for the Museum of Exp.
    Physics   R. xxxiii. 83
    of the immediate past   Pr. viii. 314
Antlers of Deer, Implements
         R. xxxiii. 19
Antoninus Pius, Coins. See *Coins,*
    Roman
Antwerp, La Maison Plantin
         C. iv. 271
Apollo, Temple of   R. xlviii. cxxxvii
Apthorp pedigree   R. xxxiii. 36
Aran Islands, co. Galway, Ethnology
    and Archaeology   Pr. viii. 358
Arbury, Camp
         R. xiii. 7; 8vo Pub. iii.
Archaeological Study, Methods and
    means of   Pr. viii. 1
Archdeacon's Book, Caius College
         R. xxv. 8
Archer, G., of Ely, Presented palstaves
    and flint implements. 1873
         R. xxxvi. 9
Architecture. See *Aachen. Anglesey*
    Priory. Bottisham. Brampton.
    Bury St Edmunds. Cambridge.
    Castle Acre. Cirencester. Com-
    berton. Deerhurst. Dover. Els-
    worth. Ely. Eton. Fahy.
    Fulbourn. Garway. Grantchester.
    Hauxton. Horham Hall. How
    House. Landbeach. Libraries.
    Lichfield. Linton. Mainz. Milton.
    Moats and Moated Halls. Mo-
    nastic buildings. Nuremberg.
    Pampisford. Prague. Shengay.
    Little Shelford. Swaffham Prior.
    Teversham. Veysy. Winchester.
    York.
Architectural Nomenclature of the
    Middle Ages, by R. Willis. 1844
         4to Pub., No. ix.
Arctic Exploration, Relics of Barentz
    at the Hague   R. xxxviii. xi

Ardoch, Perthshire, Camp Pr. vɪɪɪ. 57
Arizona, Objects from Indian cave dwellings and cliff dwellings
Pr. vɪɪɪ. 23
Arkesden, Bronze wedge R. xxxvɪ. 15
Armorial ensigns of the University and Colleges and of the Regius Professors Pr. vɪɪɪ. 107
Arms. See *Heraldry*
Arnold, General Benedict, Will, 1781
O. vɪɪ. 18
Arrow-heads from Newmarket
R. xʟɪɪ. xlii
from Pennsylvania R. xʟ. xx
from Upper Canada R. xxxvɪ. 9
Imitations of ancient flint
R. xvɪɪ. 10
Art, Fine, as applied to the illustration of the Bible Pr. vɪɪ. 31, 76
Articuli Universitatis Cantabrigiae, c. 1415 C. ɪ. 85; R. xɪv. 6
Ascham, Roger, Letters
R. xɪv. 7; C. ɪ. 99
Ashdon, Roman potter's kiln
R. xʟ. xxviii
Ashton, Dr, Letters relative to Dr Bentley C. ɪɪ. 195
Remarks...on Syriac MSS C. ɪɪ. 219
Ashwell Church, Inscription and picture R. xʟv. xvi
Music R. xxɪɪ. 7
Athena Nikephoros, Statue R. xʟɪ. xix
Athenae Cantabrigienses, Suggestions
C. ɪ. 49, 65
Specimen sheets exhibited R. xvɪɪɪ. 7
Athenian Mercury, Richard Sault, one of the editors C. ɪɪɪ. 37
Athenian Inscription R. xvɪɪ. 9
Athletic Sports illustrated by Coins
R. xʟɪv. cxxviii
Atkinson, E., Edmund Prideaux. 1890
Pr. vɪɪ. 197
Atkinson, T. D., House of the Veysy family in Cambridge. (12 plates.) 1889 Pr. vɪɪ. 93
Architectural history of Horham Hall. 1891. (3 pp. of ill.) Pr. vɪɪ. 210

Atkinson, T. D. (*continued*)
Hauxton Parish Church (on painting of St Thomas of Canterbury). 1892 Pr. vɪɪɪ. 75
Roman house at Swaffham Prior, Cambs. (1 ill.) 1893
Pr. vɪɪɪ. 229
Hall of Michael House, Cambridge. (4 ill.) 1893 Pr. vɪɪɪ. 234
Site of the Chapter House of Ely Cathedral. (1 ill.) 1893
Pr. vɪɪɪ. 242
Atkinson, T. D. and J. E. Foster, Catalogue of Loan Collection of Plate, 1895. See *Plate*
Atkinson, T. D. and T. McK. Hughes. Remains of Roman House, Swaffham Prior. 1892–3 Pr. vɪɪɪ. 173, 229
Atlantis, Legend of R. xʟɪɪɪ. lxxxvii
Aurelianus, Coins C. v. 225
Aurelius, Coins R. xʟv. vii
Australian weapons R. xʟvɪɪɪ. cxxxiv
Avenches. See *Aventicum*
Aventicum, Electrotype of a die of a Gaulish coin R. xxxɪɪɪ. 36
Axe, Bronze, from Horningsey
R. xxxvɪ. 22
Flint, from Bottisham Lode
R. xxxvɪ. 13
Flint, from Cromer R. xxxvɪ. 21
Stone, from Lake Superior
R. xxxvɪ. 9
Axes, Saxon (?), from Newmarket
R. xxxvɪ. 21
Two lacustrine R. xxxɪɪɪ. 36
Axon, W. E. A., Legend of the Chapman of Swaffham. 1883
R. xʟɪɪɪ. lxxxix
Aycliffe, Durham, Sculptured stones
Pr. vɪɪ. 17

Babington, C. C., Ancient Cambridgeshire: or an attempt to trace Roman and other ancient roads that passed through the County of Cambridge, with a record of the places where Roman coins and

Babington, C. C. (*continued*)
other remains have been found.
4 plates and 1 map. 1853.
8vo Pub. III.
Ditto. Second Edition, enlarged.
1 map. 1883   8vo Pub. xx.
Small earthen vessel found on the
site of the Roman Villa at Comberton. 1849   R. IX. 7
Cast of medallion found at Burwell.
1849   R. IX. 7
Sketch of a Saracenic Arch at Gar-
way, Herefordshire. 1849 R. x. 6
Sculptures in Rollestone church,
Herefordshire. 1849   R. x. 6
British and Roman roads in Cam-
bridgeshire. 1850   R. x. 9
Seals of Edward III. 1850 R. xi. 7
Catalogue of tradesmen's tokens
known to have been issued in the
County of Cambridge during the
latter part of the xvii. century.
1851.   C. I. 15
Roman pottery found near Foxton,
Cambs. 1 plate. 1852 C. I. 43
Four ancient ditches in the southern
part of the county. 1852
R. xii. 8
Antiquities found in Corpus College.
(1 plate and 1 ill.) 1852
C. I. 51
Roman Causeway found in Bridge
Street in 1822. 1853 R. xiii. 7
Measurements of the Camps at King's
Hedges and at Arbury. 1853
R. xiii. 7
Roman Inscriptions on the Hun-
tingdon Road. 1853 R. xiii. 7
Foss, or Devil's Ditch near Brandon;
and that near Swaffham, Norfolk.
1854   C. I. 95
Excavations of tumuli made by the
Rev. J. J. Smith, near Bincombe,
Dorsetshire, 1842. (1 plate.) 1854
C. I. 141
Supplement to his paper on the Fen
Way. 1855   R. xv. 10

Babington, C. C. (*continued*)
Imitations of ancient flint arrow-
heads and stone hammers. 1857
R. xvii. 10
Impression from a seal for labourers'
passes for the hundred of North
Stowe. 1857   R. xvii. 10
Imitations of Roman pottery. 1857
R. xviii. 7
West Mere, at Wretham, near Thet-
ford, Norfolk. 1858
C. I. 339; R. xviii. 8
Bronze falx found in the Fens. 1859.
(Ill.)   O. I. 361
Anglo-Saxon remains found near
Barrington. 1860. (1 plate.)
C. II. 7; R. xx. 8
Roman interments between Gravel
Hill farm and Howe's house.
1861   R. xxi. 8
A pair of stones, forming a grain-
rubber, from Anglesey Abbey.
1861   R. xxi. 8
Flint implements from the drift near
Amiens. 1861   R. xxii. 6
Flint hammer found near Burwell.
1862   C. II. 201
Map of Cambridgeshire, by E.
Bowen, circa 1750. 1862
R. xxii. 8
Skull of Bos Primigenius associated
with flint implements. 1863. (1
plate.)   C. II. 285
Flint 'cores' or masses from which
flint flakes have been struck.
1863   R. xxiii. 8
Roman interments by the side of the
so-called Via Devana near Cam-
bridge. 1863. (1 plate and ill.)
C. II. 289
Imitation of a leaden Pilgrim's
badge. 1863.   R. xxiv. 7
Remains of the Hospital of St John
the Evangelist in Cambridge. 1864.
(4 plates.)   C. II. 351
Two resinous seals, xvii. century.
1866   R. xxvi. 9

Babington, C. C. (*continued*)

Musea or Studiola in Dr Legge's building, Caius College. 1868. (1 plan.) C. III. 177

Roman jar from Burwell Fen. 1868 R. XXXIII. 15

Small brass figure of an ecclesiastic, found in Conington Church. 1870 R. XXXIII. 20

Discovery of a Roman villa at Hauxton. 1871 R. XXXIII. 25

Illustrations of old buildings of St John's College. 1873 R. XXXIII. 37

Bronze celt, from Bottisham Lode. 1874 R. XXXVI. 10

Flint axe and bronze spur from Bottisham Lode. 1874 R. XXXVI. 13

Palaeolithic flint axe found at Cromer. 1876 R. XXXVI. 21

Sketch of east window of the Chapel of St John's College. 1876 R. XXXVI. 21

Ancient cemetery in the grounds of G. S. Gibson, Esq., of Saffron Walden. 1876 R. XXXVI. 24

'Hoisting,' by an earthquake in Peru. 1876 R. XXXVII. x

Wat's and Offa's Dykes. 1880 R. XLI. xiv

Roman remains exhibited by Mr. Pigot. 1880 R. XLI. xvi

Roman remains at Girton and Rougham. 1881 R. XLI. xxii

Rings of annual growth of trees. 1881 R. XLII. xl

Remarks on J. C. Bruce's paper on Hadrian's Wall. 1882 R. XLII. xliii

On the death of the Rev. S. S. Lewis. 1891 Pr. VII. 287

Babington, C. C., and J. J. Smith, Foundations of buildings at Ickleton and Chesterford. 1848 R. IX. 6

Babington, Churchill, An Athenian inscription. 1856 R. XVII. 9

Babington, Churchill (*continued*)

Greek Imperial coin found in Cambridge. 1862. (Ill.) C. II. 1

Bronze celt from Horningsey. 1860 R. XXI. 6

Three coins of Carausius from Horningsey, Waterbeach, and Histon Road, Chesterton. 1861 R. XXII. 6

Unpublished coin of Carausius obtained in Cambridge, with two similar unpublished coins of Allectus. 1862. (Ill.) C. II. 235

Inscriptions copied in Crete, by Capt. Spratt. 1863 R. XXIII. 8

An inscribed gem. 1867 R. XXXIII. 7

Some silver coins of Henry VIII and Edward VI, found at Bourne. 1867 R. XXXIII. 7

Death. 1889 Pr. VII. 71

Babraham, Free Chantry C. I. 205

Bacon, Sir Francis. Election as Burgess in Parliament C. III. 203

Bacon, G. Mackenzie, An old wooden tankard. 1879. (Ill.) C. IV. 219

Medieval Jugs from Ditton. 1881 R. XLIII. xxxvi

Baines, Sir Thos., Arms at Padua. Pr. VIII. 344

Baker, Thos., MSS., Extracts relating to the election of Vice-Chancellor. R. xv. 10

Mosheim's Letter to the University. C. I. 195

On election of Vice-Chancellor, A.D. 1600 R. xv. 10

Proposed Index to MSS. by J. J. Smith and E. Venables R. II. 4, III. 5, IV. 5, VI. 4

Index to the Baker MSS., by Four Members of the Cambridge Antiquarian Society (J. J. S., C. C. B., C. W. G., J. P.) 8vo. 1848

Copy of Godwin's Catalogue of Bishops. 1615 R. XXV. 8

Notes in Newman's Concordance R. XVII. 10

Bale, Bishop, Letter to Archbishop
Parker C. III. 157
Ballycroy, co. Mayo, Plans of Fahy
Chapel R. XIV. 7
Fibula R. XXXIII. 27
Balsham, Chantry C. I. 206
Banks, S., Traces of painting in Cot-
tenham Church. 1854 R. XIV. 8
Roman bronze bust found near
Cottenham. 1855 R. XV. 9
Catalogue of subscriptions for the
relief of sufferers from the cattle-
plague, 1747, at Cottenham. 1865
C. III. 107 ; R. XXVI. 7
Irish fibula. 1871 R. XXXIII. 27
Two touchstones found in Cotten-
ham. 1871 R. XXXIII. 27
Medieval seal. 1871 R. XXXIII. 27
Denarius of Vespasian. 1871
R. XXXIII. 27
Banks' collection, Bronze helmeted
bust R. XLII. XXXV
Barbadoes, Charib implements
C. III. 295
Shell implements R. XXXVI. 22
Stone implements R. XXXVIII. xii
Barbour, John, Poems C. III. 111
Barentz, W., the Arctic Explorer,
Relics at the Hague
R. XXXVII. xi
Barnard Castle, Merchant's mark
R. XXXIII. 36
Barnham, Roman coins R. XXXVI. 10
Barnwell. See Cambridge
Baron, Stephen, Sermons R. IX. 8
Barrington, Anglo-Saxon remains
C. II. 7 ; R. XX. 8
Anglo-Saxon cemetery C. V. 5
Chantry C. I. 207
Danish remains R. XX. 8
Horse-shoe R. XXXIX. xix
Pottery rings R. XLII. li
Remains R. XXXIX. xviii; XLI. xii
Stones discovered in river
R. XLIV. cxvi
Bartlow, coins R. XL. xx
Barton, John, Notes on the past history

Barton, John (continued)
of the Church of the Holy Trinity,
Cambridge. 1879. (3 plates.)
C. IV. 313
Bassingbourne, Catalogue of church
library R. VI. 12
Churchwardens' accounts
R. XXII. 7 : XL. xxii
Vestments, etc. R. XXXIII. 11, 13
Bateman, Bp, Books given to Trinity
Hall C. II. 73
Bead, Anglo-Saxon, from Foxton
R. XXXVI. 26
Glass, from Haslingfield R. XXXIX. xii
Beads, mother-of-pearl, from Great
Shelford R. XLVI. lx
Glass, from Londesborough Park
R. XLIV. cxxix
Anglo-Saxon, from Haslingfield
R. XXXVI. 20
Beaufort, Thos., Duke of Exeter, Letter
to the University C. III. 273
Beaufort, Margaret, Countess of Rich-
mond and Derby, Vow of widow-
hood C. I. 71
Plate belonging to R. XXXIII. 19
Register containing Bp Fisher's
funeral sermon, etc.
R. XXXIII. 15
Tomb in Westminster Abbey
C. V. 267
Beccles, First Prayer-book of Edward
VI, at C. I. 67
Beck, J., Bronze gothic thurible from
Elingheims Church, in the Island
of Gothland. 1879 R. XL. xiv
Copper-ring money used in trade on
the west coast of Africa. 1881
R. XLI. xxv
Filagree ball pendants. 1881
R. XLI. xxv
Studs of belts from Iceland. 1881
R. XLI. xxv
Becket, Thos., Archbishop of Canter-
bury, Painting in Hauxton Church
Pr. VIII. 75
Bedford, Offa's Lane R. XLI. xiv

Bedfordshire Quarter Sessions Records, 1652—1662   Pr. viii. 61

Bedfordshire. See *Felmersham. Shefford. Warden*

Bell, W., Remarks on C. L. Acland's Antiquities of the immediate past. 1894   Pr. viii. 317

Bell from Newnham   R. xl. xvi

Inscription, 1294   R. xxxiii. 15

Cold Ashby   R. xxxvi. 9

See also *Horse-bell*

Bells, Church, of Cambridgeshire, by J. J. Raven. 1881. 1882

8vo Pub., Nos. xviii., xix.

belonging to King's College

C. iv. 223

Ornamented   R. xxxvi. 9

Beloe, E. M., On the port of Lynn. 1888   R. xlviii. cxl

Remarks on G. F. Browne's paper on Pampisford Church. 1888

R. xlviii. cxxxix

The great Fen road and its path to the sea. 1889. 4 plates

Pr. vii. 112

The making of Lynn. 1892

Pr. viii. 60

Beloe's Sexagenarian, Key R. xvi. 10

Belt studs from Iceland   R. xli. xxv

Bendall, C., On the monumental brass in Weston Colville Church. 1879

R. xl. xii

Bendyshe, Capt., Presented Roman pottery from Foxton. 1852

R. xii. 7

Presented Anglo-Saxon or Danish remains from Barrington. 1860

R. xx. 8

Bennet, E. K., Notes from a Norfolk Squire's Note-Book, with some particulars of school and college expenses in the xvi. and xvii. centuries. 1883

C. v. 201; R. xliii. lxxvii

Bennett, Norman, Antiquities found on Messrs Fosters' premises in Silver Street. 1892   Pr. viii. 58

Bentley, Dr Richard, Letter to Lord Chancellor King   C. iii. 175

Letters to Dr Ashton, relative to

C. ii. 195

Letters to Kuster   C. vi. 362

Letters, in Diary of Edward Rudd

8vo Pub., No. v.

Bethlehem, Roman remains

R. xxxvi. 11

Bible, Fine Art as applied to its illustration   C. vii. 31, 76

Bible prints by Rob. Whitehall, 1677

R. xxxvii. xii

Biblical History, Coins referring to

R. xlii. xlv

Bidwell, C., Romano-British Vase, part of a *patera* in Samian ware, and a *mortarium*, from Ely. 1881

R. xli. xxv

Round horse-shoes from Stuntney Fen. 1886   R. xlvi. lxxi

Bienne, Lake of, Pottery rings

R. xlii. li

Biggleswade, Roman lamp

R. xlvii. xcviii

Bilton, Stones at   R. xliv. cxxxiii

Binchester, Roman Station R. xlii. xli

Bincombe, Dorsetshire, Tumuli

C. i. 141

Birch, S., Cover of the Sarcophagus of Rameses III, in the Fitzwilliam Museum. 1875   C. iii. 371

Birkbeck, W. Ll., Remarks on O. C. Pell's paper on the Domesday Geldable Hide. 1885 R. xlv. xviii

Bishops, Godwin's catalogue, 1615; Baker's copy   R. xxv. 8

Bit, Horse, from Barrington R. xli. xii

Bithynia, Portrait of Homer upon an unpublished coin of Nicaea in

C. v. 41

Black Death, Inscription at Ashwell

R. xlv. xvi

Black earth pits near Cambridge

R. xxxvi. 25

Black oak from Burwell Fen

R. xxxiii. 36

Blomfield, A. W., Account of St Vigor's Church, Fulbourn, enlarged and restored. 1870. (4 plates.) C. III. 215

Blood, Human, in vase from Anstey R. XXXVIII. xviii

Blooteling, Abraham, Picture belonging to R. XVI. 9

Bodger, J. W., Coins and other objects found at Peterborough. 1890 Pr. VII. 189

Bois, John, Letters, 1611 C. II. 139

Bologna, Sculptured stones R. XLVII. cxii

Bone. See Implements, Matrix

Bones, Human, from Burwell R. XLIV. cxxvii; XLVII. civ

from Fen Ditton R. XXXVII. xii

from Great Ormeshead R. XXXIII. 8

Bonney, T. G., Flint Implements found near Amiens. 1863 R. XXIII. 8

Recent discoveries among the Pfahlbauten at Concise, Lake of Neufchatel. 1864 R. XXV. 7

Flint weapon from Haslingfield. 1865 R. XXVI. 7

Proclamation concerning Popish recusants. 1865 R. XXVI. 7

Dutch snuff-box. 1865 R. XXVI. 7

Megalithic remains in South Brittany. 1866 R. XXVI. 8

Earthenware amphora, from Chesterton. 1867 R. XXXIII. 7

Flint weapons from Denmark. 1867 R. XXXIII. 8

Ancient iron key from Willingham. 1867 R. XXXIII. 8

Shells and bones, with fragments of burnt clay &c., from Great Ormeshead, N. Wales. 1867 R. XXXIII. 8

Two Letters of Sir Isaac Newton. 1867 C. III. 153 ; R. XXXIII. 8

Implements made of antlers of red deer. 1869 R. XXXIII. 19

Bookcases, Fragments of the XVII. century, at Clare College C. VIII. 18

Medieval Libraries with special reference to R. XLV. xxxviii

See also Libraries, Library

Book-clasps from Chesterton R. XLI. xiii

Books printed on vellum in the University and Colleges of Cambridge, by S. Sandars. 1878 8vo Pub., No. XV.

in medieval collegiate libraries, System of storing and delivering R. XXXVII. ix

See also Catalogue

Booth, Robt., Letters to Dr Claiton and Dr Gwyn C. I. 343 : II. 139

Bos longifrons, Remarks on R. XLV. xi

Bos primigenius, from Wilburton, Horns R. XLV. xvii

Horns R. XL. xx

Skull associated with flint implements C. II. 285

Bottisham, History and antiquities of the parish, by E. Hailstone, 1873–8 8vo Pub., Nos. XIV., XVI.

Bottisham Fen, Seal R. XXXIII. 20

Bottisham Lode, Celt R. XXXVI. 10

Bottle, Glass, 'Thomas Ewin, Cambridge, 1736' R. XLV. vii

Glass, from site of Post-Office R. XLV. xvi

Leathern, with specimens from Mr Redfern's collection Pr. VIII. 60

Pilgrims', from site of Post-Office R. XLV. xiii

Pilgrim's leaden R. XXXIII. 16

Medieval, from Newmarket R. XLIII. lxxvii

of white ware, from Croydon R. XXXIII. 31

probably Phoenician R. XXXVI. 15

Bottles, Glass, from Garlic Fair Lane R. XXXIX. xvi

from Gravel Hill Farm C. II. 289

Boundary Walls, Manor House and College   C. iii. 287
Bourne, Coins   R. xxxiii. 7
Chantry   C. i. 207
Bouth, Robert. See *Booth*
Bowen, Emm., Map of Cambridgeshire, c. 1750   R. xxii. 8
Bowes, R., Biographical notes on the University Printers from the commencement of printing in Cambridge to the present time. 1884. (107 ill.) C. v. 283, Remarks by A. P. Humphry   R. xliv. cxxii
The Cambridge University Press, 1701-7 (John Owen). 1887 C.vi.362
On J. Siberch. 1890   Pr. vii. 189
On the death of Rev. S. S. Lewis, 1891   Pr. vii. 288
The first and other early Cambridge Newspapers. 1894   Pr. viii. 347
Bowl, Crystal, representing a Wyvern   Pr. viii. 390
Bowl of Samian ware   R. xlvii. cxii
Boxford, Parish accounts   R. xvii. 9 ; C. i. 265
Boxworth, Chantry   C. i. 208
Bradshaw, Hen., Lyfe of St Radegund, *circa* 1520   C. i. 29
Bradshaw, H., Broadsheet lamentation on the death of Henry VIII. 1859   R. ix. 7
Account of the Trinitarian House in Cambridge, from Lopez's History. 1861   R. xxi. 8
List of books which belonged to Canterbury Cathedral a.d. 1170–1180. 1861   R. xxi. 9
A copy on vellum of the earliest Primer printed in England, probably a.d. 1494. 1861 R. xxi. 9
Richard Croke, Public Orator, 1519–25. 1861   R. xxi. 9
Recovery of the long-lost Waldensian Manuscripts. 1862   C. ii. 203
Two lists of books in the University Library, 1473 and 1424. 1862   C. ii. 239

Bradshaw, H. (*continued*)
Extracts from the Cellurar's Register of Bury Abbey. 1862 R. xxiii. 8
Early University Statutes concerning Hostels. 1863   C. ii. 279
Transcript of the process of the Papal Legates in the case of the divorce between Henry VIII and Katherine of Arragon. 1864   R. xxiv. 7
Wood-engraving of the xv. century, pasted in a book printed at Cologne, 1477. 1866. R. xxvi. 8
A volume of Calendars, 1477, believed to be the earliest book with engravings on copper. 1866.   R. xxvi. 8
Two hitherto unknown poems by John Barbour, author of the Brus. 1866   C. iii. 111
View of the state of the University in Q. Anne's reign. 1866. (1 plate)   C. iii. 119
The earliest English engravings of the Indulgence known as the 'Image of Pity.' 1867. 1 plate (facsimile)   C. iii. 135
Inventory of the stuff in the College Chambers, King's College, 1598. 1868   C. iii. 181
An iron shackle. 1868   R. xxxiii. 15
Bronze dagger found in Burwell Fen. 1870   R. xxxiii. 21
Engraved device used by Nicolaus Gotz of Sletzstat, the Cologne printer, in 1474; with a note on a book printed at Cologne by Gotz in 1477, with two illustrations engraved on copper. 1870   C. iii. 237
Two engravings on copper, by G. M., a wandering Flemish artist of the xv.-xvi. century. 1870   C. iii. 247
Note A. Three engravings on copper, fastened into the Cam-

Bradshaw, H. (*continued*)
 bridge copy of the Utrecht
 Breviary of 1514 C. III. 255
 Note B. Engravings fastened
 into the Lambeth copy of the
 Salisbury Primer or Horae,
 printed by Wynkyn de Worde,
 about 1494 C. III. 257
 The oldest written remains of the
 Welsh language. 1871
 C. III. 263
 Exhibition of a complete series of
 the Forms of Commemoration of
 Benefactors used by authority in
 the University Church, since the
 first half of the XVII. century.
 1872 R. XXXIII. 31
 Portraits belonging to the University
 before the Civil War. 1872
 C. III. 275
 Notes of the episcopal visitation of
 the Archdeaconry of Ely, 1685.
 1875 C. III. 323
 The ABC as an authorised school-
 book in the XVI. century. 1875
 C. III. 363
 The earliest extant example of
 printing. 1876 R. XXXVII. ix
 The Light of St Erasmus, and on
 the various spellings of his name
 in the Trinity parish accounts.
 1879 C. IV. 327
 Remarks on Units of measurement
 in Domesday. 1881
 R. XLII. xxxviii
 Remarks on R. Bowes' paper on the
 University printers. 1884
 R. XLIV. cxxii, cxxiii
 Remarks on Cambridge Libraries.
 1885 R. XLV. xxxviii
 Death, 1886 R. XLVI. liii
Brampton Church, Hunts., Choir-
 stalls Pr. VII. 28
Brandon, Ditch C. I. 95
Brandon flint-trade R. XLV. xxxiii
Brass, Rubbing, with date '29 Feb.
 1629' R. XLI. xxii

Brass (*continued*)
 in Toft Monks Church R. XL. xxiv
 in Weston Colville Church, c. 1430
 R. XL. xii
 of Anstey R. XVI. 10
 Palimpsest, in Burwell Church
 R. VII. 3
Brasses, Rubbings R. IX. 6
 in Little Shelford Church
 R. VIII. 6
 Monumental, foreign R. XLVI. lix
 Palimpsest sepulchral, by Sir A. W.
 Franks 4to Pub., No. XIV. part 1
 Palimpsest (1) Peter Rede, (2) Eras-
 mus Paston, 1530. R. XII. 8
Bray, Wm., Letter from Dr Ed.
 Martin C. II. 149
Brazil. See *Rio Janeiro*
Brent Pelham, Visitation of the
 Church C. III. 53
Breviary, Utrecht, 1514. Engravings
 in the Cambridge copy C. III. 255
Brick, Triangular, from Hunsbury .
 R. XLVI. lxxiv
Bricks, Triangular, found near North-
 ampton R. XLVI. lxix
British Coins. See *Coins*
British Merlin for 1751 R. XVII. 10
British Museum, Essex MSS.
 R. XVI. 10
 Graeco-Egyptian Papyrus C. I. 37
 Two fragments of Acts of Martyrs
 Chamoul and Justus C. I. 191
 Sculptured stones R. XLIV. cxxxii
British remains. See *Jar, Shield,
 Vase*
British roads in Cambridgeshire
 R. X. 9
Brittany, Megalithic remains in South
 R. XXVI. 8
Bronze and stone implements
 R. XXXVI. 24
Brocklebank, T. Sir Robert Rede.
 1859 R. XIX. 8; C. I. 365
 Extracts from Wills preserved at
 King's College. 1860 R. XX. 8
 Exhibited (1) a silver medal by D.

Brocklebank, T. (*continued*)
Hood of Cambridge, 1796, (2) a
brass piece of James II. 1867
R. xxxiii. 11
Letter from Peter Salmon, M.A.,
to Samuel Collins, D.D., Provost
of King's College, written from
Padua, 1630. 1870 C. iii. 211
Bronze implements &c. from Arkesden
R. xxxvi. 15
Brittany R. xxxvi. 24
Burwell Fen R. xxxiii. 31
Ely and Swaffham R. xlvii. xcviii
Hauxton R. xlviii. cxxxvi
Newmarket R. xlv. xxii
near Royston R. xlviii. cxxxviii
See also *Axe, Celt, Dagger, Spear-
head*
Bronze ornament on vessel from Farn-
dale R. xxxiii. 30
Brooch from Barrington R. xli. xii
near Royston R. xlviii. cxxxviii
Brough-under-Stanmore, Inscription
R. xlv. xxiii
Browne, G. F., Sections of two holes
lined with clay, formerly used for
cooking purposes, at Great Hal-
lingbury, Essex. 1874
R. xxxvi. 11
Ivory figures, mostly Flemish. 1875
R. xxxvi. 20
Handle and portion of a knife from
Schloss Heideck. 1875
R. xxxvi. 20
A silver figure. 1875 R. xxxvi. 20
Silver reliquaries. 1875
R. xxxvi. 20
A medallion, French. 1875
R. xxxvi. 20
Hobson's House 'the White Horse'
and Mr Cory's House. 1876
C. iii. 405
Sculptured stones and crosses in the
North of England. 1882
R. xliii. lxxiii
Similarity of some ornamental scrolls
in the mausoleum of Galla Placida

Browne, G. F. (*continued*)
at Ravenna to some sculptured
stones in England. 1883
R. xliii. lxxviii
Sculptured stones in Lothian, and
in Durham and Yorkshire. 1883
R. xliv. cx
Sculptured stones in the British
Museum, and the Guildhall, Lon-
don, and other stones. 1884
R. xliv. cxxxii
Inscriptions and supposed inscrip-
tions. 1884. (2 plates) C. vi. 1
Inscribed stone from Brough-under-
Stanmore. 1885 R. xlv. xxvii
Stone Cross-head presented by the
Royal Architectural Museum to
the Society. 1885 R. xlvi. lvii
xv. century Italian Casket. 1885
R. xlvi. lxii
Sculptured stones and symbols in
Ledsham Church, Yorkshire. 1886
R. xlvi. lxvi
Triangular bricks found near North-
ampton. 1886 R. xlvi. lxix
Sculptured columns at Stapleford,
Notts. and Rothley, as bearing on
the dedication of places. 1886
R. xlvi. lxxii
Triangular pierced brick from Huns-
bury. 1886 R. xlvi. lxxiv
The later vestments of St Cuthbert's
body, about 1100. 1886
R. xlvii. xciv
An ivory plaque from Elmham.
1886. R. xlvii. c
Figure from a crucifix, found at Ceres
in Fife, 1886. R. xlvii. ci
Drawings of the martyrdom of St
Erasmus. 1886 R. xlvii. cii
On M. Rule's paper on Deerhurst
Church, 1886 R. xlvii. ciii
Sculptured crosses at Heysham,
Halton and Winwick. 1887
R. xlvii. cv
Address on retiring from the Pre-
sidency. 1887 R. xlvii. cxi

Browne, G. F. (continued)
Sculptured stones in Rome, Ravenna, Bologna, and Mantua.
1887 R. xlvii. cxii
Figure of a saint from Guilden Morden. 1888. R. xlviii. cxl
The Tympanum of the South door of Pampisford Church, and the Rectory of Pampisford. 1888. 1 plate
C. vi. 384; R. xlviii. cxxxix
Sculptured stones (Fulbourn; Catterick and Croft, Yorks; and Aycliffe, Durham). 1889
Pr. vii. 17
On E. Magnússen's Stone of Jaellinge. 1889 Pr. vii. 23
Sculptured stone with a Runic Inscription from Cheshire. 1889
Pr. vii. 86
Sculptured stone with an Ogam Inscription. 1889 Pr. vii. 88
The old altar-slab of St Benedict's Church, Cambridge. 1889. (2 illustrations in text) Pr. vii. 89
Exhibited plate of figures of inscribed stones of Scotland. 1890
Pr. vii. 131
Browning, O., Keltiberian Inscription in the theatre of Saguntum. 1881
R. xli. xxiii
xvi. century Spur from Scurgola. 1881 R. xli. xxv
Bruce, J. Collingwood, Hadrian's Wall. 1882 R. xlii. xliii
Drawings of coins referring to Biblical History. 1882 R. xlii. xlv
Brunswick, Bronze figure of a lion
R. xxxvi. 16
Ancient onyx known as the Mantuan Vase C. iii. 307
Buckenham, Fresco R. xlvii. cii
Bucket at ancient well at Mountsorrel
Pr. viii. 133
Buckinghamshire. See Whaddon Chase
Budge, E. A. W., Egyptian Antiquities. 1887 R. xlvii. cx

Budge, E. A. W. (continued)
Syriac and Coptic versions of the martyrdom of St George of Cappadocia. 1890 Pr. vii. 133
Burgh, Chantry C. i. 208
"Burienge of Great Persons," MS.
R. xxii. 6
Burleigh, Wm. Cecil, Lord, Signature and Seal R. xix. 8
Burmanni itineris Anglicana acta diurna R. xxii. 8; xxv. 8
Burwell, Bones and fibula
R. xliv. cxxvii
Flint hammer C. ii. 201
Human bones R. xlvii. civ
Medallion R. ix. 7
Tobacco stopper R. ix. 7
Burwell Church, Palimpsest brass
R. vii. 3
Burwell Fen, Black oak R. xxxiii. 36
Bronze implement R. xxxiii. 31
Bronze dagger R. xliii. lxxii
Roman jar R. xxxiii. 15
Red-deer horn R. xxxiii. 36
Skeleton of Red Stag R. xlv. xxx
Bury St Edmunds, The Abbey of, by M. R. James. 1895
8vo Pub., No. xxviii
Abbey, Cellarar's Register
R. xxiii. 8
Bury St Edmunds fair, Tract on
R. xviii. 8
Bust, Bronze helmeted, from the Banks Collection R. xlii. xxxv
from near Royston
R. xlviii. cxxxviii
in Roman glass-paste, Intaglio, probably of Prince Charles Edward
R. xxxvi. 22
Roman bronze, from Cottenham
R. xv. 9
Bysshe, Sir Thos., Seal R. xiii. 6

Caesar, Julius, Coins. See Coins: Roman
Caistor, Lincolnshire, Coins
R. xl. xiv, xxii

Caius College. See *Cambridge*
Caldecote, Bell   R. xxxvi. 9
Mill-stone   R. xliv. cxxvii
Calendar, Ancient, in Library of Jesus
  College   C. i. 147
Norwegian   C. iv. 129
Runic, found in Lapland C. iv. 17
Calendars, Runic, Four   C. vi. 368
  with copper engravings, 1477
                         R. xxvi. 8
Calverley, William and Walter, of
  Clare Hall   R. xxv. 10
CAMBRIDGE:
Antiquities found at   R. xx. 7;
  xxxii.11; xxxvi.25; xlii. xxxix;
  xlviii. cxl.; Pr. viii. 74, 292
Bone matrix   R. xiii. 6
Bottles   R. xxxix. xvi
Drinking vessels   R. xxxii. 20
Fibula   R. xxv. 10
Finger-ring   R. xliii. lxxxiii
Flint implements   R. xl. xiii
Horse-shoe   R. xli. xxv
Key   R. xxxiii. 16
Knife   R. xxvi. 10; xxiii. 7
Lamp   R. xli. xiii
Pin   R. xli. xiii
Pocillum   R. xxxiil. 27
Pottery   R. xxxiii. 11, 13, 16;
  xxxviii. xi; xlii. 2; xlv. xiii;
  Pr. vii. 1.
Urns   Pr. viii. 282
Vases   R. xxxiii. 20; xlii. L
Objects acquired by the Museum
                         R. xlvii. xcviii, cxiii
Armorial Ensigns of the University
  and Colleges and of the Regius
  Professors   Pr. viii. 107
Application of Heraldry to the
  illustration of University and
  Collegiate Antiquities, by H. A.
  Woodham. 1841-2. Plates
             4to Pub. Nos. iv. and v.
Articuli Universitatis Cantabrigiae,
  c. 1415   C. i. 85.
Athenae Cantabrigienses.
             R. xviii. 7; C. i. 49, 65

CAMBRIDGE (*continued*)
Aula de Wimpole between the Great
  Bridge and St John's   R. xxiii. 8
Babington, C. C., Ancient Cam-
  bridgeshire 8vo Pub. Nos. iii, xx.
Barnwell, Brass Signet R. xxxvi. 16
Cylindrical stone   R. xxxiii. 13
Flint implement   C. iv. 177
Hobblers from Gravelhole
                         R. xxxiii. 27
Barnwell Priory, Architectural His-
  tory   Pr. vii. 222
Moat and Hall   C. iii. 287
Books printed, 1521-1700
                         R. xxxiii. 8, 9
Bridge Street, Roman Causeway
                         R. xiii. 7
Caius College, Archdeacon's Book
                         R. xxv. 8
Musea or Studiola in Dr Legge's
  building   C. iii. 177
Canopy carried over Q. Elizabeth at
  Cambridge, 1564   Pr. vii. 194
Castle, Two stone coffins R. xiii. 6
Castle Hill   Pr. viii. 173
Castle Hill, Token of the 'Three
  Tuns,' near   R. xxxiii. 26
Cavendish College, Coin found
                         R. xliv. cvii, cxxiv
Chancellor's Gold Medal, 1810
                         R. xxxiii. 20
Chantries and Free Chapels
                         C. i. 209
Christ's College, Curiosities (forged)
                         R. xxxiii. 25
Fireplace in Master's Lodge
                         C. vi. 374
Civil Law Faculty, Petition for re-
  storation   R. xix. 7
Clare College, Bird's-eye view, 1714
                         Pr. vii. 197
Clare College, Fragments of xvii.
  century book-cases Pr. viii. 18
Coins, Tokens and Medals of the
  Town, County and University, by
  W. G. Searle. 1871
             8vo Pub., No. xii

CAMBRIDGE (*continued*)

Coins found   R. xxiii. 7; xxxiii.
    33; xxxviii. xix; xlv. lx;
            C. ii. 1, 235
Coins struck at   R. xxvi. 7
Coldham Common, Pottery
        R. xxxiii. 11: xxxviii. xi
College Expenses, xvi. and xvii. cen-
    turies   C. v. 201
Commemoration of Benefactors,
    Forms   R. xxxiii. 31
Corpus Christi College, Antiquities
    found at   C. i. 51
Catalogue of Books given by Thos.
    Markaunt, 1479, edited by J. O.
    Halliwell. 1847
            4to Pub., No. xiv.
Parker MSS. Evangelia Augustini
    Gregoriana. Edited by J. Good-
    win. 1847   4to Pub. No. xiii.
Lewis Collection. See *Lewis Col-
    lection*
Costume in the University
            R. ix. 7, 8
Ditches between Hobson Street and
    Sidney Street   Pr. viii. 32
    near the Pitt Press   Pr. viii. 255
Documents relating to, during the
    Commonwealth   R. xxi. 7
Emmanuel College. Greek Psalter
    in Library   Pr. viii. 168
Life of Dr Laurence Chaderton
            R. xliv. cxxix
Esquire Bedell, The third R. xiii. 7
Esquire Bedell, and Yeoman Bedell,
    Maces   C. iv. 207
Fairs. See *Sturbridge Fair*
Fitzwilliam Museum, Stones from
    Via Appia   R. xliv. cxxxv
Sarcophagus of Rameses III
            C. iii. 371, 383
Garlic Fair   Pr. viii. 113
Garlic Fair Lane (Park Street),
    Bottles   R. xxxix. xvi
Garlic Row   Pr. viii. 313
Garrett Hostel Green, Enclosure
            Pr. vii. 261

CAMBRIDGE (*continued*)

Gonville and Caius College. See *Caius*
Heraldry. See *Armorial*
High Stewards of the University,
    The earlier   C. i. 273
History of, Books
        R. i. 5; ii. 6; iii. 6; iv. 7
History of, MSS.
        R. i. 6; ii. 10; iii. 6; iv. 7
History of, MSS., Desirability of
    publication   R. xv. 10
Hobson, Thos., Deed   R. xx. 8
House in Trumpington Street
            C. iii. 405
Hobson Street, Ditch   Pr. viii. 32
Hospital of St John, Remains
            C. ii. 351
Seal   R. xiii. 7
Exemptions from duties to Church
    of All Hallows   R. xxxiii. 18
List of plate, 21 Hen. VIII.
            R. xxxiii. 19
Sketch of east window of Chapel
            R. xxxvi. 21
Hostels, University statutes con-
    cerning   C. ii. 279
Huntingdon Road, Bone implement
            R. xxxiii. 13
Roman pottery   R. xxxiii. 13
Roman inscription   R. xxxiii. 13
Gravel Hill Farm, Roman inter-
    ments   R. xxi. 8
Installation Medal of Prince Albert
            R. xxxiii. 27
Inscriptions, Roman
        R. xiii. 7: xxxiii. 13
Jesus College, Calendar preserved in
    Library   C. i. 147
Chapel, Recent discoveries
            R. xliii. lxxxvi
Coins   R. xxiii. 7
Drinking vessel (xvi. century)
            R. xxxiii. 20
Pocket-knife from garden
            R. xxiii. 7
Jesus Lane, Storey's Almshouses
            R. xxxiii. 27

CAMBRIDGE (*continued*)

King's College, Chapel, Bells

        C. iv. 223

 Chapel, Orientation C. i. 59

 Deed granting Arms R. ix. 6

 Inventory of Stuff in College

  Chambers, 1598 C. iii. 181

 Notaries Public   C. iii. 47

 Old Provost's Lodge C. iv. 285

 Records : Manumissions of Serfs

        C. i. 359

 William Milligan, First Provost

        C. i. 287

 Wills at   R. xx. 8

King Street, Vases R. xlii. 2

Ditches   Pr. viii. 32

Law Schools R. xlvi. lxxiv

Libraries, Bibliography of Cambridge, by S. Sandars

    8vo Pub., No. xv.

See also under the various Colleges.

Maces in the University Registry

     R. xxxix. xiv

Maces of the Esquire Bedells and

 Yeoman Bedell C. iv. 207

Madingley Road, Roman pottery

       Pr. vii. 1

 See also the *Observatory*

Market Hill, House of the Veysy

 family   Pr. vii. 93

Michael House, Hall Pr. viii. 234

Midsummer Common, Pottery

       R. xx. 7

Mill Road, Flint implements

       R. xl. xiii

Monuments to Cambridge men at

 Padua   Pr. viii. 337

Museum of Experimental Physics,

 Antiquities R. xxxiii. 33

Newspapers, The first and other

 early   Pr. viii. 347

Observatory, Coin found

     R. xxxviii. xix

Romano-British Urns

      R. xxxix. xi

Park Side, Horse-shoes R. xli. xxv

Park Street. See *Garlic Fair Lane*

CAMBRIDGE (*continued*)

Parliament of, 1388 C. i. 281

Election of Burgesses for the University to the second Parliament

 of James I.   R. xiv. 7

Election of Sir F. Bacon and Dr

 Goche as Burgesses, 1614

      C. iii. 203

Choice of Burgesses for the University, 1611 R. xx. 7

Pembroke College, Books presented

 in the xiv. and xv. centuries

       C. ii. 11

Ground plan of the Studiola

    R. xxxix. xviii

MS. of the New Testament in

 Latin, in Library Pr. viii. 221

Peterhouse, Consecration of Chapel

 by Archbishop Sancroft

      R. xxiv. 8

One Shilling of James I., found in

 Lodge garden R. xlv. lx

Petty Cury, Origin of the name

       C. i. 63

House of the Veysy family

       Pr. vii. 93

Pin and Lamp R. xli. xiii

Pottery from site of Post-Office

      R. xlv. xiii

Pitt Press, Ancient ditches near

      Pr. viii. 255

Plan, by Hamond, 1592 C. vii. 13

Plays, Dr Legge's Richardus Tertius,

 1579–80.   C. i. 347.

Poem on...varieties of the most

 renowned University, 1673

      R. xxiv. 8

Portraits belonging to the University before the Civil War

      C. iii. 275

Post-Office. See *Petty Cury*.

Queens' College, Earliest Accounts

 and Inventories R. xvii. 10

Earliest Bursar's accounts

      R. xviii. 9

Catalogue of the Library in 1472

      C. ii. 165

CAMBRIDGE (*continued*)

History of, 1446–1662, by W. G.
Searle. 1867-71
8vo Pub., Nos. ix., xiii.
Inventory of Plate sent to K.
Charles I, 1642　　　C. 1. 241
Letter from Dr E. Martin, Presi-
dent　　　　　　　　C. 1. 149
St Andrew the Great, Chalice for-
merly belonging to church
R. xli. xviii
St Benedict's Church, Altar slab
C. vii. 89
St Catharine's College, Foundation
of　　　　　　　R. xviii. 8
Catalogue of the original Library,
1475, by G. E. Corrie. 1840
4to Pub., No. i.
Robert Woodlark, Founder and
first Master　　　C. 1. 329
St Edward's, Original Documents
relating to the parish　C. iv. 358
St John Baptist, History of the
church　　　　　　C. iv. 343
Original documents relating to
parish and church　C. iv. 358
St John Zachary. See *St John Baptist*
St John's College, Actors in Legge's
Richardus Tertius, 1579-80
C. 1. 347
Bone matrix　　　R. xiii. 6
Chapel. Sketch of the East win-
dow　　　　　　R. xxxvi. 21
Cinerary Urns　　Pr. viii. 282
Controversy with Trinity College
Pr. vii. 261
Documents from the Treasury
R. xxxiii. 18, 19
Bp Fisher's papers in the Treasury
R. xxiv. 8
Goods belonging to, 1520-1544
R. xxiii. 7
Illustrations of Old Buildings
R. xxxiii. 37
Letter-book　　　R. xxv. 9
Letter to the Countess of Shrews-
bury　　　　　　C. 1. 47

CAMBRIDGE (*continued*)

Letters of Robert Bouth and John
Bois in the Treasury C. ii. 139
Letters of Robert Booth to Dr
Claiton concerning the Second
Court　　　　　　C. i. 343
Letters from Wren and Hawks-
moor, on proposed new bridge
Pr. vii. 254
Library, Descriptive Catalogue of
MSS. and Scarce Books, by M.
Cowie. 1842-3
4to Pub., Nos. vi. and viii.
Library, Letters and building ac-
counts　　　C. ii. 25, iii. 61
Plans and other documents, con-
cerning the Second Court
R. xxxiii. 15
Remains, from A.-S. cemetery at
backs　　　　　R. xlviii. cxl
Remains found under two elms in
grounds　　　R. xlii. xxxix
Statutes, First set　R. xxxiii. 16
Tragedy of Richardus Tertius per-
formed　　　　　C. i. 347
See also *Hospital of St John*
St Mary the Great, Church, His-
torical and Architectural Notes,
by S. Sandars, together with
Annals of the Church, by E.
Venables. 1869 8vo.Pub., No. x.
Original Indenture for erection of
rood-loft, 1521　R. xxxiii. 16
St Mary's Passage, Pottery
R. xxxiii. 16
St Michael's Church. Register of
Births, Marriages and Deaths,
1538-1837, edited by J. Venn.
1891　　　8vo Pub. No. xxv.
Portrait of Charles I. in Vestry
R. xlii. xxxvii
St Radegund's Priory, Charters
Pr. viii. 309
Schools' Quadrangle　R. xliv. cxvi
Sidney Sussex College, Account of
the Old Chapel, by James Essex
R. xxxviii. xvi

CAMBRIDGE (*continued*)

Sidney Sussex College, Dr Johnson's legacy R. xxiii. 9

Silver Street, Antiquities Pr. vii. 58

State of the University in Q. Anne's reign C. iii. 119

Storey's Almshouses. See *Jesus Lane*

Sturbridge Fair, Tract R. xviii. 8

Garlic Fair Pr. viii. 313

Garlic Row Pr. viii. 313

Tokens of the Town, University and County, by W. G. Searle. 1871 8vo Pub., No. xii.

Tokens of "Three Tuns" R. xli. xii; xxxiii. 26

Town Court, Gift or render of a Sore Hawk: (21 Ed. III.) C. i. 169

Trinity Church, Notes on the past history C. iv. 313, 327

Effigy of a Bishop R. xl. xiii

Trinity College, Architectural History of Neville's Court R. xliii. lxxxii

Biographical Notes on the Librarians of Trinity College, by R. Sinker. 1897 8vo Pub., No. xxix

Controversy with St John's College Pr. vii. 261

Hall and Chapel in 1702 R. xxv. 8

Library, Leaden vessel R. xxxix. xiv

Redmayne's MS. Life of Henry V. R. xxi. 8

Runic Inscription C. vi. 313

Objects of antiquarian interest Pr. viii. 292

Objects found in an attic R. xlv. xxxi

On the site of R. xlii. xlix

Walks, Enclosure Pr. vii. 261

Trinity Hall, Books given by the Founder C. ii. 73

Excavations R. xl. xxi

CAMBRIDGE (*continued*)

Trinity Hall, Token R. xli. xii

"Warren's book": Extracts R. xl. xxi

Trumpington Road, Dam Hill, Roman Remains R. xl. xxi

Trumpington Street, Hobson's House; the White Horse, or "Germany"; and Mr Cory's House C. iii. 405

See also *Pitt Press*

University, Letter from Duke of Exeter C. iii. 273

University Commissary's Proceedings, 1579–1600. MS. R. xxxvi. 23

University Library, Two lists of books, 1424 and 1473 C. ii. 237

MS. Psalter Pr. viii. 146

Contribution of Colleges for the Librarian R. xxi. 7

University Printers, 1521 to 1884, Biographical Notes C. v. 283

See *John Owen, John Siberch*

University Registry, List of documents, 1266–1544 C. iii. 285

Maces R. xxxix. xiv

Verses on the University, MS. R. xix. 7

Vice-Chancellor, Election of, 1600 R. xv. 10

Visit by Burmann R. xxii. 8, xxv. 8

Visit by Uffenbach, 1710 R. xxii. 6

Woodwardian Museum, Stone weapons R. xxxviii. xii

CAMBRIDGESHIRE:

Ancient, by C. C. Babington. 1853 8vo Pub., No. iii.

Second Edition, enlarged. 1883 8vo Pub., No. xx.

Assessments, 1291–1889 Pr. viii. 55

Chantries and Free Chapels C. i. 201

Church Bells of, by J. J. Raven, and Supplement. 1881–2 8vo Pub., Nos. xviii. and xix.

CAMBRIDGESHIRE (*continued*)

Coins, Tokens and Medals of the
Town, County and University of
Cambridge, by W. G. Searle.
1871   8vo Pub., No. xii.
See also C. C. Babington's
Ancient Cambridgeshire

Ditches, Four ancient, in southern
part of the County   R. xii. 8
referred to by Tacitus
Pr. vii. 200

Domesday, Measurements and valuations   C. v. 93

Heralds' Visitations   C. ii. 67

Inquisitio Comitatus Cantabrigiensis   C. vi. 45 ; R. xlv. ix.

King's Hedges, Camp   R. xiii. 7

Map, by Bowen, *circa* 1750
R. xxii. 8

Nonae Rolls   C. i. 7

Notes of parishes, from Liber Archidiaconi Eliensis   R. xxxiii. 7

Pedes Finium : a short calendar of
the Feet of Fines, by W. Rye.
1891   8vo. Pub., No. xxvi.

Roads, Roman and British R. x. 9
See C. C. Babington's *Ancient
Cambridgeshire*

Survey of Manors in the County
Pr. vi. 17

See *Abington Pigotts. Anglesey
Abbey. Babraham. Balsham.
Barrington. Bartlow. Bottisham.
Bourne. Boxworth. Burgh. Bur-
well. Caldecote. Cambridge.
Chatteris. Cherryhinton. Ches-
terton. Clopton. Cottenham.
Chippenham. Coveney. Ditton.
Dry Drayton. Elsworth. Ely.
Eversden. Fordham. Foxton.
Fulbourn. Girton. Grantchester.
Guilden Morden. Hardwick. Has-
lingfield. Hauxton. Histon.
Horningsey. Isleham. Kirtling.
Landbeach. Linton. Littleport.
Malketon. Malton. Manea.
March. Meldreth. Milton. New-*

CAMBRIDGESHIRE (*continued*)

*ham. Newton. Orwell. Over.
Papworth Everard. Quy. Roys-
ton. Sawston. Shelford. Shepreth.
Stow. Steeple Morden. Stretton.
Stuntney Fen. Swaffham Bul-
beck. Swaffham Prior. Swavesey.
Teversham. Trumpington. Water-
beach. Westley Waterless. Weston
Colville. Whittlesford. Wilbraham.
Wicken. Willingham. Wimpole.*

Cameo of Marcia as Omphale
C. v. 233

representing Jupiter Dodonaeus
C. v. 183

Camp at Ardoch, Perthshire
Pr. viii. 57
at King's Hedges and Arbury
8vo Pub., iii. and xx.
in Wiltshire, &c.
R. xlv. xiv.; xlvi. lxxi

Canada, Upper, Stone implements
R. xxxvi. 9

Canoe found in the Ouse Marshes
C. iv. 195 ; R. xxxix. xiii
from the Pacific Islands
R. xlviii. cxxxiv
Sakit   Pr. vii. 289

Canopic Jar   R. xliv. cxxxi

Canopy carried over Queen Elizabeth
at Cambridge, 1564   C. vii. 194

Canosa, Andro-sphinx R. xxxvi. 22

Canterbury, Ancient Library at Christ
Church   Pr. viii. 359

Cathedral, Books belonging to, A.D.
1170–1180   R. xxi. 9
pavement   R. ix. 7

Canton, Stone implements
R. xxxviii. xii

Capaneus, The fall of: an Etruscan
Intaglio   C. vi. 378

[Caraccioli, Charles], Tract on Bury St
Edmund's and Sturbridge Fairs
R. xviii. 8

Carausius, Coins. See *Coins: Roman*

Car Dyke, from Peterborough to Cambridge   R. xii. 8

Carlisle, Roman inscription
    Pr. VIII. 85
Carnac, Flint and chalcedony
    R. XXXVI. 24
Carreg-lab   R. XXXVIII xii
Carter, Jas., 'Wool' weight belonging
to Saffron Walden Museum. 1865
    R. XXV. 9
Holed-stone from Chesterton. 1865
    R. XXV. 9
Bronze fibula found near the gas-
works at Cambridge. 1865
    R. XXV. 10
Vases found on Coldham Common.
1867   R. XXXIII. 11
Roman vase found on the Hunting-
don Road. 1868   R. XXXIII. 13
Bone implement found on the Hun-
tingdon Road. 1868
    R. XXXIII. 13
Stone hammer found at Swaffham
Fen. 1868   R. XXXIII. 15
Pilgrim's leaden ampulla with ar-
morial bearings. 1869
    R. XXXIII. 16
Flint implement of bronze form im-
ported from Denmark. 1870
    R. XXXIII. 20
Flint implements of the palaeolithic
age from Chatteris. 1873
    R. XXXVI. 9
Excavations, apparently of Roman
date, recently discovered at Ful-
bourn. 1875   C. III. 313
Silver ring XIV. cent. R. XXXVII. xiii
Leaden vessel found at Willingdon,
Sussex. 1879   R. XXXIX. xviii
Carving, Ivory R. XXXII. 20; XLVII. c
Casket, Italian, XV. cent.
    R. XLVI. lxii
Steel, from Nuremberg R. VIII. 6
Castell-y-Mynach, Glamorganshire,
Wood in ruins   Pr. VIII. 93
Castle Acre, Norfolk, The Cluniac
Priory   Pr. VIII. 243
Catalogue of Bishops, Godwin's
    R. XXV. 8

Catalogue of Books given to Trinity
Hall by the Founder C. II. 73
given to Corpus College by Thos.
Markaunt, 1439. Edited by J. O.
Halliwell
    4to Pub., No. XIV., Part 3
in Canterbury Cathedral, A.D. 1170–
1180   R. XXI. 9
presented to Pembroke College
    C. II. 11
and MSS. in St John's College
Library, by M. Cowie. 1842-3
    4to Pub., Nos. VI. and VIII.
in the University Library, Cambridge, 1424 and 1473 C. II. 239
in the Church Library, Bassingbourne   R. VI. 12
in the Church Library, Swaffham,
Norfolk   R. VI. 12
in the Library at Queens' College
    R. XXII. 7
in the Library, Revesby Monastery
    R. XVI. 10
in the original Library of St Catharine's College, 1475, by G. E.
Corrie   4to Pub., No. I.
Catharine, St, of Alexandria, Historical
inquiry touching, by C. Hardwick.
1849   4to Pub., No. XV.
Catharine of Aragon, Process of Papal
Legate in divorce of R. XXIV. 7
Catterick, Yorks., Sculptured stones
    Pr. VII. 17
Cattle-plague at Cottenham, 1747,
Subscriptions for relief
    C. III. 107
Cave dwellings and cliff dwellings in
Arizona   Pr. VIII. 23
Caxton, Millstone R. XLIV. cxxxvii
The "moats" at R. XLIII. lxxxiii
Roman horse-shoe R. XLIII. lxxxiii
Cellurar's Register of Bury Abbey
    R. XXIII. 8
Celts, Bottisham Lode R. XXXVI. 10
Horningsey   R. XXI. 6
Littleport   R. XLI. xiv
Swaffham Fen   R. XLIV. cxxix

Celts (*continued*)
Teversham   R. xxxvi. 11
Thetford   R. xlvii. xcvii
Tours   R. xxxviii. xix
naturally formed, from Icklingham
                   R. xlii. xlii
Celtic Coins   C. vii. 189
Cemetery, Ancient, at Saffron Walden
                   R. xxxvi. 24
See *Anglo-Saxon. Roman*
Ceres, Fife, Crucifix   R. xlvii. ci
Ceres, Head of Livia as, from a gem
                   R. xxxiii. 36
Cæena, Chained library   Pr. viii. 1
Chaderton, Dr Laurence, Life
                   R. xliv. cxxix
Chalcedony from Carnac R. xxxvi. 24
Chalice, formerly belonging to Rock-
land Church   R. xli. xviii
formerly belonging to St Andrew's
Church, Cambridge R. xli. xviii
Chamoul and Justus, Acts of C. i. 191
Channel Islands, Land measures in
                   C. vi. 305
Chantries and Free Chapels C. i. 201
Chapman, H., Four letters of Charles I.
                   R. vi. 12
Chapman, F. R.   Purchase of the
manor and advowson of Mepal in
the xiv. century, by the Prior and
Convent of Ely, 1890 Pr. vii. 131
Chapman of Swaffham, Legend
                   C. iii. 317; R. xliii. lxxxix
Chapter House of Ely Cathedral
                   Pr. viii. 242
Charib implements in Barbadoes
                   C. iii. 295
Charibs, Origin and usages of the
                   R. xxxvi. 11, 22
Charles I., Letters   R. vi. 12
Portrait   R. xx. 8
Portrait in St Michael's Church
                   R. xlii. xxxvii
Memorials of the Stuarts
                   R. xlii. xxxvii
Charles I. and II., Forms of Prayer at
coronations   R. xxiv. 8

Charles Edward, Prince, Intaglio bust
                   R. xxxvi. 22
Charterhouse, Roman signets found
in lead mines   C. iv. 277
Chasubles from Sawston Hall
                   Pr. vii. 10
Chatelaine, Gold   R. xxxvi. 11
Chatteris, Flint implement
                   R. xxxvi. 9
Chaucer's Troilus and Cressida, ms.
                   C. vi. 331
Cherryhinton, Newly discovered dyke
                   Pr. viii. 317, 322
Cheshire, Sculptured stone with a
Runic inscription Pr. vii. 86
Cheshire. See *Whitley*
Chesterford, Great, Foundations of
buildings   R. ix. 7
Roman remains
   R. xxxiii. 24; xlii. liv; xlv. xii
Vase   R. xxxvii. xiii
Excavations R. xl. xvi, xxiv, xxvii
Roman Kiln
                   R. xxxix. xvii; xl. xxvii
Chesterton, Amphora   R. xxxiii. 7
Book-clasp   R. xli. xiii
Church, Fresco
                   C. iv. 37; R. xxxviii. xi
Coin of Carausius   R. xxii. 6
Farthing   R. xlv. xxxi
Flint implements from gravel-pits
                   R. xl. xiii
Objects   R. xxxviii. xvi
Perforated stone   R. xxv. 9
Tokens   R. xxxvi. 22; xli. xii
Chinese Coins. See *Coins*
Chippenham Church, Mural paintings,
&c.   R. xlvii. cii; C. vi. 321
Choir-stalls from Brampton Church
                   Pr. vii. 28
Christ's College. See *Cambridge*
Church furniture at Brent Pelham
                   C. iii. 53
and vestments at Bassingbourne
                   R. xxxiii. 11 and 13
Church and parochial libraries
                   C. i. 33

Churchwardens' accounts at Bassingbourne R. xxii. 7; xl. xxii
Leverton, Lincolnshire R. xxv. 8
Churton, W. R., Legend of St George the Martyr. 1890 Pr. vii. 135
Cirencester, Roman buildings C. i. 55
Cissbury, Stone implements and pottery R. xxxvi. 10
Remains R. xxxvi. 26
Cistercian Abbey of Revesby; Catalogue of Library R. xvi. 10; C. i. 97
Monastery at Whitwick R. xlviii. cxxxvii
Citeaux, Ancient Library Pr. viii. 359
Clairvaux, Ancient Library Pr. viii. 359
Claiton, Dr Richard, Master of St. John's College, Letters from Rob. Booth C. i. 343
Clare College. See Cambridge
Clark, E. C. The Minster Church at Aachen, and St Vitale, Ravenna. 1882 R. xlii. xlix
on B. Walker's paper on Ancient Camps in Wiltshire. 1884 R. xliv. xvi
Inscribed stone from Brough-under-Stanmore. 1885 R. xlv. xxiii
Symbols in Ledsham Church. 1886 R. xlvi. lxvii
The Law School, from 1470. 1886 R. xlvi. lxxiv
on C. W. King's paper on a tablet in Trinity College Library. 1886 R. xlvii. xciii
on T. McK. Hughes' paper on Earthworks between the Solway and the Tyne. 1887 R. xlviii. cxxxiv
on E. G. de S. Wood's paper on Stamford University. 1888 Pr. vii. 2
H. Gadow's Early Christian Inscription. 1888 Pr. vii. 8
W. Ridgeway's paper on Cambridgeshire Ditches. 1891 Pr. vii. 207
on the death of the Rev. S. S. Lewis. 1891 Pr. vii. 286

Clark, E. C. (continued)
Methods and means of Archaeological study. 1891 Pr. viii. 1
Roman inscription at Carlisle. 1892 Pr. viii. 85
An Etruscan inscription at Perugia. 1893 Pr. viii. 253
on T. McK. Hughes' paper on Ancient Ditches. 1893 Pr. viii. 282
Exhibits a leather bottle, with three specimens from Mr W. B. Redfern's collection. 1894 Pr. viii. 60
Garlick Fair. 1894 Pr. viii. 313
on C. L. Acland's paper on Antiquities of the immediate past. 1894 Pr. viii. 317
British jar found at Haslingfield. 1894 Pr. viii. 331
Clark, J. W. Historiola Collegii Corporis Christi, by J. Josselin. 1880 8vo Pub., No. xvii.
Description of the Medrásen in Algeria. 1875 C. iii. 379
Bronze axe from Horningsey. 1876 R. xxxvi. 22
Shell implements from Barbadoes. 1876 R. xxxvi, 22
Bronze statuette, Egyptian. 1876 R. xxxvi. 22
System adopted for storing and delivering books in medieval collegiate libraries. 1876 R. xxxvii. ix
Josselin's Historiola Coll. Corporis Christi. 1877 R. xxxvii. xii
Chained Psalter or Horae, written for John Harpur of Russhale, Staffs., in xv. century. 1878 R. xxxviii. xvi
History of the peal of Bells belonging to King's College, Cambridge. 1879. (1 plate) C. iv. 223
Suggestions as to the best mode of preserving the two Maces in the Registry. 1879 R. xxxix. xiv
Glass bottles from Garlic Fair Lane. 1879 R. xxxix. xvi

Clark, J. W. (continued)

The site of Trinity College. 1882
R. XLII. xlix
The old Provost's Lodge of King's College, with special reference to the furniture. 1879. (1 plan)
C. IV. 285
(List of the most uncommon words occurring in the accounts, p. 310)
History of the Church of St John the Baptist, Cambridge, commonly called St John Zachary. 1879. (1 plan) C. IV. 343
Appendix of original documents, 1444–1453, relating to the parishes of St Edward and St John the Baptist, and the Church of St John, from Trinity Hall muniment room and elsewhere, p. 358
Origin of 'Mutton-Hole.' 1882
R. XLII. xlix
Architectural history of Neville's Court, Trinity College. 1882
R. XLIII. lxxxii
Monuments of Central America. 1883 R. XLIII. lxxxviii
Tomb of Margaret Beaufort, Countess of Richmond and Derby, in Westminster Abbey. 1883 C. V. 265
Address as President. 1883, 1885
R. XLIV. cvii; XLV. xxxv
on G. F. Browne's paper on Sculptured stones in Lothian. 1883
R. XLIV. cvi
The Schools quadrangle, Senate-house. 1883 R. XLIV. cxvii
on A. P. Maudslay's Explorations in Central America. 1883
R. XLIV. cxx
on R. Bowes' paper on University Printers. 1884 R. XLIV. cxxii
Human bones and part of a fibula from Burwell. 1884 R. XLIV. cxxvii
Description of the loan collection of Portraits. 1884 R. XLIV. cxxix

Clark, J. W. (continued)

Two varieties of Ox. 1884
R. XLV. xi
Skeleton of a Red Stag (Cervus elaphus) from Burwell Fen. 1885
R. XLV. xxx
on H. F. Wilson's Objects of interest from Trinity College. 1885
R. XLV. xxxi
Medieval Libraries, with special reference to book-cases. 1885
R. XLV. xxxviii
on J. R. Clouting's paper On a Skull. 1886 R. XLVII. xcviii
Part of a human skeleton from Burwell. 1887 R. XLVII. civ
Notes on a fireplace discovered in the Master's lodge, Christ's College. 1888. (1 plate) C. VI. 374
Skeleton of a stag (Cervus elaphus) from Manea Fen. 1888 Pr. VII. 2
Exhibits a sheet of Hamond's plan of Cambridge, 1572. 1889
Pr. VII. 13
The canopy carried over Q. Elizabeth when she visited Cambridge, 1564. 1890 Pr. VII. 194
Bird's-eye view of Clare Hall, 1714. 1890. (1 plate, and 1 ill.)
Pr. VII. 197
Architectural history of Barnwell Priory. 1891. (1 plate, and ill.)
Pr. VII. 222
Death of the Rev. S. S. Lewis. 1891
Pr. VII. 289
on T. McK. Hughes' paper on Ancient Ditches. 1893 Pr. VIII. 282
Chained Libraries at Cesena, Wells, and Guildford. 1891. (1 plate and 10 ills.) Pr. VIII. 1
Fragments of XVII. century bookcases at Clare College, Cambridge. 1891. (3 ills.) Pr. VIII. 18
on A. Gray's Charters of the Priory of St Radegund. 1894
Pr. VIII. 313
Ancient Libraries: (1) Christ Church,

Clark, J. W. (*continued*)
  Canterbury; (2) Citeaux, Clairvaux;
  (3) Zutphen, Enkhuizen. 1894.
  (2 plates and 13 ills.)
              Pr. viii. 359
  Catalogue of the first Exhibition of
  University and College Portraits
  held in the Fitzwilliam Museum,
  May 1884
  Catalogue of the second Exhibition
  of University and College Portraits
  held in the Fitzwilliam Museum,
  May 1885
Claudius, Coin   C. v. 225
Clay, W. K. History of the parish of
  Waterbeach, (3 plates). 1859
          8vo Pub., No. iv.
  Landbeach, (1 plate). 1861
          8vo Pub., No. vi.
  Horningsey. 1865
          8vo Pub., No. vii.
  Milton. 1869   8vo Pub., No. xi.
  Notes on parishes in Cambridgeshire,
  from the 'Liber Archidiaconi Eli-
  ensis' in Caius College Library.
  1867   R. xxxiii. 7
  death. 1867   R. xxxiii. 9
Clay, Fragment of burnt, from Great
  Ormeshead   R. xxxiii. 8
Climacus, Johannes, Scala, 1475
          Pr. vii. 17
Clock, Brass   R. xxxiii. 26
Clock-case from near Royston
     R. viii. 5; xxxiii. 26
Clog, Plate of,   C. i. 51
Clopton, Chantry   C. i. 210
Clouting, J. R. Skull and celt from
  Thetford. 1886 R. xlvii. xcvii
Clugny, Deed of Convent of, with farm-
  ers of Offord, 1237 R. xlvii. cx
Cluniac Priory at Castle Acre
          Pr. viii. 243
Cobham, Eleanor, Duchess of Glou-
  cester. Lament...when convicted
  of sorcery   C. i. 177
Coenwulf, King of Mercia, Coin
          R. xxxvi. 25

Coffins, Stone, found near the Castle
          R. xiii. 6
Coinage. Suggestions for a Coinage
  for Ireland and other Islands be-
  longing to England, by N. Tyery.
  Edited by G. O. White-Cooper and
  F. J. H. Jenkinson. 1886. (32
  ills. in text). 8vo Pub., No. xxii.
Coining and the Implements of Coin-
  ing   C. iv. 109
Coins from Caistor, Lincolnshire
          R. xl. xxii
  Chesterford   R. xxxix. xviii
  Smyrna   R. xliv. cxxxviii
  Woodstone Hill   Pr. vii. 189
  referring to Biblical history
          R. xlii. xlv
  struck by the Crusaders
          R. xxxiii. 11
Coins, Catalogue of, Roman and Eng-
  lish Series, in the Museum of the
  Society. 1847. 8vo.
Coins :
  American : U. S. Dollar, 1795, and
  Confederate States Dollar note
          R. xxxiii. 35
  Anglo-Saxon
    Harthacnut   R. xxiii. 7
    Bavarian   R. xxvi. 8
    British
      Cunobelinus
        R. xxxviii. xvi ; xlv. xxxi
      Tincommius   R. xl. xxvii
      Verica   R. xl. xxvii
    Celtic   C. vii. 189
    Chinese R. xxxiii. 16 ; xxxvi. 11
    English, from Hitchin Pr. vii. 152
    Coins, Tokens and Medals of the
    Town, County and University
    of Cambridge, by W. G. Searle.
    1871   8vo Pub., No. xii.
    Silver, from Shefford, Beds
        4to Pub., No. x. page 24
    Channel Island type R. xl. xiv
    Chesterton farthing R. xlv. xxxi
    Coenwulf   R. xxxvi. 25
    Edward III.   R. xxiii. 7

Coins, English (*continued*)

Edward VI.   R. xxxiii. 7
George III.   R. xxxvi. 15
Henry II.
    R. xxiii. 7; xxxix. xii, xvi
Henry VI.   R. xiii. 8
Henry VIII.   R. xxxiii. 7
James I. R. xlii. xxxvii; xlv. ix
James II.
    R. xxxiii. 11; xxxix. xii
Perkin Warbeck   R. xl. xx
Victoria   R. xxxvi. 15
William and Mary R. xxxvi. 15
French R. xxxiii. 31, 36; xxxviii. xi
Gaulish R. xxxiii. 35; xxxvi. 10;
     Pr. vii. 135
German   R. xxvi. 8; xxxiii. 37
Greek Imperial   C. ii. 1
Macedonian
    R. xxxiii. 35; C. vii. 189
Macedonian as illustrating the
  degeneracy in athletic games
     R. xliv. cxxviii
Nicaea   R. xx. 7; C. v. 41
Selinus   R. xliv. cxxviii
Haytian   R. xxi. 6
Hebrew: Shekels   R. xxxvi. 17;
     xxxvii. ix; C. vi. 12
Indian, 1833   R. xxxiii. 35
Japanese   R. xxxiii. 16, 36
Mexican   R. xxxiii. 36
Roman:
from Shefford, Beds
     4to Pub., No. x.
Collection from Commodus to
  Constantine II.   R. xxxvi. 10
Collection from Domitian to Septi-
  mus Severus   R. xxxvii. xiii
Collection from Gallienus to Con-
  stantinus Jun.   Pr. vii. 189
Collection from Nero to Gordia-
  nus III.   Pr. vii. 189
Allectus   C. ii. 235
Antoninus Pius   R. xxxvii. xiii;
     xliii. lxxxvii; Pr. vii. 189
Aurelius   R. xlv. vii
Aurelianus   C. v. 225

Coins, Roman (*continued*)

Bronze, iv. century Pr. vii. 185
Julius Caesar   R. xxxiii. 36;
     Pr. vii. 189
Carausius R. xxii. 6; C. ii. 235
Claudius   C. v. 225
Constans   R. xlv. xxxi
Constantinus Max. R. xxxiii. 16,
  36; xxv. 10; xliii. lxxxvi; xlviii.
  cxxxvi; Pr. vii. 189
Crispina, Empress R. xxxiii. 33
Diocletianus   C. v. 225
Faustina the yr.   Pr. vii. 189
Gallienus R. xli. xi; C. v. 225
Gratianus
    R. xlv. xxxi; xlviii. cxxxvi
Hadrian R. xxxiii. 33, 37; xliv.
    cxxi; xlviii. cxxxvi
Laelianus   C. v. 225
Magnentius   R. xl. xvii
Marius   C. v. 225
Maximianus Hercules
    R. xlii. lxxvii; xliv. cxxi
Nero   R. xxxvii. ix
Nero Drusus   R. xlv. xxxi
Nerva   R. xlviii. cxxxvi
Postumus   C. v. 225
Probus R. xxxviii. xix; C. v. 225
Sabina, Empress R. xliii. lxxxvi
Salonina, Empress   C. v. 225
Saloninus   C. v. 225
Severina, Empress   C. v. 225
Severus   R. xliv. cvii
Tacitus   C. v. 225
Tetricus C. v. 225; R. xl. xx
Tetricus jun.   C. v. 225
Trajanus R. xiv. 6; xliii. lxxi;
    xliv. lviii, cvii, cxxiv
Valens   R. xliii. lxxvii
Valentinianus   R. xl. xvii
Vespasianus   R. xxxiii. 27
Victorinus C. v. 225; R. xli. xi;
    xl. xvii, xx
Spanish   R. xiii. 7
Colchester, Roman pottery kiln
     R. xl. xxvii
Cold Ashby, Bell   R. xxxvi. 9

College Expenses xvi. and xvii. centuries   C. v. 201

Colleges. See *Cambridge*

Collett, W. R., Fresco-paintings formerly in Stoke Church, Suffolk. 1849   R. ix. 8

Collins, Samuel, Provost of King's College, Letter from Peter Salmon   C. iii. 211

Cologne, Book printed by N. Gotz, 1497   C. iii. 244

Cullen ware jug, xvi. cent.   Pr. vii. 169

Colquhoun, Sir P., The true site of Dodona. 1881   R. xli. xxiii

Columbaria, Manor House and College, etc.   C. iii. 287

Colvin, S., Drawings by John Flaxman. 1876   R. xxxvii. x

Comberton, Roman villa   R. ix. 7

Compton, Lord Alwyne, Drawings of pavement in the Exchequer Chamber at Exeter. 1847   R. vii. 4

Concise, Lake of Neuchatel, Discoveries among the Pfahlbauten   R. xxv. 7

Conington, Bronze figure of Mercury   R. xl. xvi

Brass figure found in Church   R. xxxiii. 20

Constans, Coin   R. xlv. xxxi

Constantine, Triumph of   C. iv. 391

Constantinus, Max., Coins. See *Coins, Roman*

Conybeare, J. W. E., Brooch, bit, knives, etc., from Barrington. 1880   R. xli. xii

Stones discovered in the river bed at Barrington. 1883   R. xliv. cxvi

Cooking, Two holes lined with clay used for, at Hallingbury   R. xxxvi. 11

Cooper, C. H., Matrix of the seal of Sir Thos. Bysshe. 1852   R. xiii. 6

Bone matrix in St John's College. 1852   R. xiii. 6

Cooper, C. H. (*continued*)

Two stone coffins found near the Castle. 1852   R. xiii. 6

Origin of the name Petty Cury, as applied to a street in Cambridge. 1853   C. i. 63

The vow of widowhood of Margaret, Countess of Richmond and Derby (foundress of Christ's and St John's Colleges) : with notices of similar vows in the xiv., xv., and xvi. centuries. 1853   C. i. 71

Letter from Oliver Cromwell to his sister Elizabeth, with notes. 1853   C. i. 81

Notices of a gift or render of a Sore Hawk, with especial reference to a fine levied in the Town Court of Cambridge, 21 Edw. III. 1855   C. i. 169

Abraham Blooteling's engraving of James, Duke of Monmouth. 1855   R. xvi. 9

Inventory of Plate sent to Charles I by Queens' College, and receipt for moneys advanced for his service by the President and Fellows, 1642, with notes. 1856   C. i. 241

The earlier High Stewards of the University. 1857   C. i. 273

Exhibits sheets of his Athenae Cantabrigienses. 1857   R. xviii. 7

Actors in Dr Legge's tragedy of Richardus Tertius, performed at the Bachelors' Commencement, 1579-80. 1858   C. i. 347

Heralds' Visitations of the County of Cambridge. 1860   C. ii. 67

Redmayne's MS. Life of Henry V in Trinity Library. 1861   R. xxi. 8

Autograph of Sir H. Spelman, with some facts respecting him. 1861   C. ii. 101

John Norris, founder of the Norrisian Professorship. 1861   C. ii. 147

Cooper, C. H. (continued)
Letter from Dr Edward Martin,
President of Queens' College, to
William Bray, Chaplain to Arch-
bishop Laud. 1861   C. II. 149
Henry Stokes, Newton's school-
master. 1862.
C. II. 161; R. XXII. 8
Feoffment from Thos. Hobson to
Thos. Newman of premises in
Cambridge. 1862   R. XXII. 8
Draft of a conveyance in 1780 of the
house in Cornhill, London, in
which the poet Gray was born.
1862   R. XXIII. 7
Agnes, Lady Wenman, translator
of Zonaras. 1863   C. II. 327
Richard Dunthorne, Astronomer,
Engineer and Antiquarian artist.
1863   C. II. 331
A recently published selection from
the wills of eminent persons.
1864   C. II. 337
Account of Richard Sault, Mathe-
matician, and one of the Editors
of the 'Athenian Mercury.' 1864
C. III. 37
An annotated copy of Godwin's
Catalogue of Bishops, 1615, for-
merly belonging to T. Baker.
1864   R. XXV. 8
Extract from the Churchwardens'
accounts of Leverton, Lincoln-
shire. 1865   R. XXV. 8
Life of Robert Hare. 1865
R. XXV. 9
William and Walter Calverley of
Clare Hall. 1865   R. XXV. 10
The establishment of printing in
New England. 1865   R. XXVI. 7
death, Remarks by J. E. B. Mayor.
1866   R. XXVI. 3
Coptic version of the martyrdom of
St George.   Pr. VII. 133
Copyright, Letter from Dr Goodman
to Dr Gwynne concerning
R. XX. 7

Cordeaux, W. W., Three British coins
from Caistor, Lincolnshire. 1880
R. XL. xiv
Bell from Newnham. 1880
R. XL. xvi
Bronze spear-head from Walton-on-
Thames. 1880   R. XL. xxii
Coins from Caistor, Lincolnshire.
1880   R. XL. xxii
Anglo-Saxon fibula-mould from Lin-
coln. 1881   R. XLI. 19
Roman pottery and other objects
from Great Cotes, in N.-E. Lin-
colnshire. 1882   R. XLII. xlvii
Corinium. See Cirencester
Coronations of Charles I and II, Forms
of prayer   R. XXIV. 8
Corpus Christi College. See Cam-
bridge
Corrie, G. E., Catalogue of the original
library of St Catharine's Hall,
1475. 1840   4to Pub., No. 1.
Prodigies recorded in history. 1847
R. VIII. 4
Changes of Costume in the Univer-
sity. 1849   R. IX. 7, 8
A rare volume of Sermons by Stephen
Baron. 1849   R. IX. 8
Copy of a minute of proceedings at
the election of representatives of
the University to the second
Parliament of James I. 1854
R. XIV. 7
Two Catalogues of monastic library
(Cistercian Abbey of Revesby).
1854   C. I. 97; R. XIV. 7
An ancient Calendar preserved in
the library of Jesus College. 1855
C. I. 147; R. XV. 9
Transcript of part of a Catalogue of
the Library of Revesby Monastery,
Lincolnshire. 1856   R. XVI. 10
Parish accounts of Boxford, Suffolk,
1529—1596. 1857   C. I. 265
Early copy of a petition for the
restoration of the Civil Law
Faculty. 1859   R. XIX. 7

Corrie, G. E. (*continued*)

Answer to a petition of Ralf Widdrington. 1859　R. xix. 8

The choice of Burgesses for the University in 1611. 1859
R. xx. 7

Petition of Journeymen Printers. 1859　R. xx. 7

List of books presented to Pembroke College by various donors during the xiv. and xv. centuries. 1860
C. ii. 11; R. xx. 7

Will of Dr Thos. Lane, Master of St Peter's College, 1431–37. 1860
R. xx. 7

Indulgence for Dr Lane and his sister, before 1437. 1860 R. xx. 7

Documents relating to the University and Town during the Commonwealth. 1861 R. xxi. 7

Facsimile of a document drawn up by Cranmer against the Pope's jurisdiction. 1861　R. xxi. 7

Papers relating to contributions from the Colleges for the University Librarian, 1654. 1861 R. xxi. 7

Catalogue of books given to Trinity Hall by the founder. 1861
C. ii. 73

A pocket-knife found in the garden at Jesus College. 1862
R. xxiii. 7

Coins from Jesus College. 1862
R. xxiii. 7

Letters addressed to Dr Ashton, Master of Jesus College, relative to Dr Bentley's candidature for the Regius Professorship of Divinity. 1862　C. ii. 195

Remarks by Dr Ashton, Master of Jesus College : (1) On the age of a Syriac MS. of the Pentateuch, (2) Gloucester Ridley's account of a Syriac MS. of the New Testament. 1862　C. ii. 219

Documents connected with the Episcopal Church in Scotland in

Corrie, G. E. (*continued*)

the reign of Q. Anne. 1862
C. ii. 225

Reasons for the completion of Dr Tudway's Degree in Music, 1705. 1862　C. ii. 345

death referred to by G. F. Browne. 1885　R. xlvi. lvii

Costume in the University, Changes of　R. ix. 7, 8

Cotes, Gt., Roman pottery
R. xlii. xlvii

Coton, Moat and Hall　C. iii. 287

Cottenham, Cattle plague : subscriptions for relief, 1747
C. iii. 107; R. xxvi. 7

Chantry　C. i. 210

Painting in church　R. xiv. 8

Roman bust　R. xv. 9

Touchstones　R. xxxiii. 27

Cottenham Fen, Roman coins
R. xliv. cvii

Court Rolls of the Manor of Littleport in the Isle of Ely　C. iv. 97

of Stow-cum-Quy　R. xvii. 10

Coveney Fen, Shields　R. vii. 4

Cowell, E. B., Legend of the Chapman of Swaffham in Norfolk. 1875. C. iii. 317. Note by W. E. A. Axon.　R. xliii. lxxxix.

A MS. volume of University Commissary's proceedings, 1599–1600. 1876　R. xxxvi. 23

Cowie, M., Descriptive Catalogue of the MSS. and Scarce Books in the library of St John's College, Cambridge. 2 parts. 1842–3
4to Pub., Nos. vi. and viii.

Cranmer, Archbp, Personal history
R. xv. 9

Paper against Papal jurisdiction
R. xxi. 7

Creeny, W. F., On Foreign monumental brasses. 1885 R. xlvi. lix

Crete, Inscriptions　R. xxiii. 8

Crimea, Earthen rampart at Perekop, at entrance to the　C. v. 47

Crispina, Empress, Coin
R. xxxiii. 33
Croft, Yorks., Sculptured stones from
Pr. vii. 17
Croke, Richard, Public Orator, 1519–
25 R. xxi. 9; xxii. 7
Cromer, Flint axe R. xxxvi. 21
Cromwell, Elizabeth, Letter from
Oliver Cromwell to his sister
C. i. 81
Cromwell, Oliver, Letter to his sister
Elizabeth C. i. 81
Crook in the hand of Rameses III on
the cover of his sarcophagus in
the Fitzwilliam Museum
C. iii. 383
Crooked lands, Existence and cause
R. xlvi. lxi
Crosby Ravensworth, Tumuli
R. xlv. xii
Cross at Sawston R. xliii. lxxvi
Cross, Processional R. xxxiil. 20
Crosses and stones from N. of England,
Sculptured R. xliii. lxxiii
Sculptured, at Heysham, Hatton,
and Winwick R. xlvii. cv
Croydon, Roman pottery R. xxxiii. 31
Croyland Abbey, Origin and date of
Ingulf's History of Pr. vii. 207
Ingulf and the Historia Croylanden-
sis, by W. G. Searle. 1894
8vo Pub., No. xxvii.
Crucifix, Figures from, in Museum
R. xlvii. c
from Ceres, Fife R. xlvii. ci
Cudworth, Ralph, Letter relating to
the life of, by J. T. Mosheim, 1727
C. i. 195
Cullen (Cologne) ware jug, xvi. century
Pr. vii. 169
Cumberland, Ring dial Pr. vii. 185
Maiden Way C. vi. 41
Cuneiform Inscription at Nineveh
R. xliii. lxxxiii
Cunningham, G., Teeth of early
Egyptian skulls. 1887
R. xlvii. cx

Cunningham, W., Land measurements
in Domesday. 1884 R. xlv. x
Bedfordshire Quarter Sessions Re-
cords, 1650–60. 1892 Pr. viii. 61
Cunobelinus, Coin
R. xxxviii. xvi; xlv. xxxi
Cuthbert, St, Vestments
R. xlvii. xciv
Cyprus, Pottery R. xl. xx

Daggers from Burwell Fen
R. xxxiii. 21: xliii. lxxii
Dam Hill, Cambridge, Roman re-
mains R. xl. xxi
Danish remains from Barrington
C. ii. 7; R. xx. 8
Darwin, G. H., Monuments to Cam-
bridge men in the University of
Padua. (4 plates) 1894
Pr. viii. 337
Death, John, Vases, probably xv.
century, from King Street. 1882
R. xlii. l
Deck, A., Pottery (Romano-British ?),
from Chesterton Road. 1868
R. xxxiii. 11
Bronze celt from Teversham. 1874
R. xxxvi. 11
Fibulae and beads from Hasling-
field. 1875 R. xxxvi. 20
Forceps found under King's Parade.
1875 R. xxxvi. 20
Horse-bell from Haslingfield. 1878
R. xxxix. xi
Deck, I., Necklace of rough amber, &c.,
from Wilbraham. 1848 R. viii. 6
Keys found in St Martin's Priory,
Dover. 1848 R. ix. 7
Dedication of Places R. xlvi. lxxii
Deed of Convent of Clugny and farmers
of Offord, 1237 R. xlvii. cx
Deeds at Wilbraham Parva, 1439 to
1646 R. xlviii. cxxxviii
Deer, Red, horns from Burwell Fen
R. xxxiii. 15
Implements made of antlers of
R. xxxiii. 19

Deerhurst Church   R. xlvii. cii
Font   R. xliv. cxxxiii
Delta, Mummy's treasures recently
    discovered in the   C. iv. 385
Dengain brass in Quy Church
    R. xvi. 10
Denmark, Flint implements imported
    from   R. xxxiii. 20
    Stone implements   R. xxxiii. 8
Derby, Margaret, Countess of Rich-
    mond and. See *Beaufort*
Devil's Ditch, near Brandon   C. i. 95
Devonshire. See *Pilton*
Dial, Pendant   Pr. vii. 135
    Ring. See *Ring-dial*
Diocletianus, Coin   C. v. 225
Disney, John, Seal of John Milton
    R. xii. 8
    Ring, c. 1450   R. xii. 8
Dispensations from Rome
    R. xxxiii. 15
Diss, Fibula   R. xliii. lxxxvi
Distances, Table of...between towns
    given by Holinshed   C. iv. 259
Ditch near Brandon   C. i. 95
    near Swaffham, Norfolk   C. i. 95
Ditches, Cambridgeshire   R. xii. 8
    Cambridgeshire, referred to by Taci-
    tus   Pr. vii. 200
    in Cambridge   Pr. viii. 32, 255
Ditton, Fen, Bones and pottery
    R. xxxvii. xii
    Coins   R. xliii. lxxxvii
    Flint-flakes   R. xxxvi. 24
    Medieval jugs   R. xlii. xxxvi
    Moat and Hall   C. iii. 287
    Perforated stone and stag's horn
    R. xl. xxvii
    Pottery   R. xlii. xxxvi
    Pottery and stone implements
    R. xliv. cxxix
    Roman and other remains
    R. xxxvi. 24
Dodona, Site of   R. xli. xxiii
Dolmens   R. xxxvi. 24
Domesday, Land Measurements
    R. xlii. xxxviii; xlv. ix, xx

Domesday (*continued*)
    Some terms used in   C. vi. 17, 65
    of Cambridgeshire, Measurements
    and Valuations   C. v. 93
Dordogne, Stone implement from
    R. xxxviii. xix
Dorsetshire. See *Rincombe*
Douay, List of subscriptions to Con-
    vent of English Franciscans at,
    1630–49   R. xxi. 9
Dover, Keys from, and pillar in St
    Martin's Priory   R. ix. 7
Downham Field, Ely, Pottery
    R. xlii. xlvii
Downing family and property
    R. xxxiii 8
Drake, C. B., Wall-paintings in Tever-
    sham Church. 1882
    R. xliii. lxxii
Drake, W. Tyrwhitt., Almandine gar-
    net set in gold. 1875
    R. xxxvi. 17
    Shekels of the time of Ezra. 1875
    R. xxxvi. 17
Dryden, Sir H., Roman and Romano-
    British remains at or near Shefford,
    Beds. 4 plates. 1845
    4to Pub., No. x.
    Plans of Fahy Chapel, Ballycroy, co.
    Mayo   R. xiv. 7
    Saxon fibulae from Newnham,
    Northants   R. xiv. 7
Dry Drayton, Chantry at   C. i. 201
Duckett, Sir G., Deed of agreement
    between the Convent of Clugny
    and the Farmers of Offord, Hunts.
    1887   R. xlvii. cx
Duckworth, W. H. L., A newly dis-
    covered dyke at Cherryhinton.
    1894   Pr. viii. 322
Duff, E. Gordon, A hitherto unknown
    book printed by John Lettou.
    1890   Pr. vii. 190
Duffield, A. J., Pre-historic Peruvian
    stone implements. 1 plate. 1876
    C. iv. 13
Dugdale, Sir Wm., Letter   R. xix. 8

Dunham, Seal of Prebend of R. xiii. 6

Dunthorne, Richard C. ii. 331

Duport, Dr, Account of Election, written by C. iii. 203

Durham, Sculptured stones R. xliv. cx

See *Aycliffe*. *Barnard Castle*

Dutch inscription in St Mary's Church, Haddiscoe R. xl. xxiv

records at the Hague R. xxv. 9

snuff-box R. xxvi. 7

Dutton, H., Description of Medieval merchants' mark, and remarks on seals of the same period. (2 ill.) 1878 C. iv. 187

Dyer, Wm., License, 1653-4. R. xxi. 7

Dyke at Cherryhinton Pr. viii. 317, 322

Dykes. See *Offa's Dyke* and *Wat's Dyke*

Eadgyth, Tomb R. xxiii. 8

Eadmer's "Historia Novorum in Anglia," On C. vi. 195

Ear-ring, Roman, from Lakenheath R. xlv. vii

Illustration of C. iv. 385

Earith, Bronze statuette found C. iii. 231

Earth-pits, Black, near Cambridge R. xxxvi. 25

Earthquake, Hoisting by an, in Peru R. xxxvii. x

Earthworks between the mouth of the Tyne and the Solway C. vi. 355

Edmund, St, Abbey of. See *Bury St Edmunds*

Edward the Elder, Tomb of Eadgyth, daughter of R. xxiii. 8

Edward the Confessor, MS. Life R. xiv. 7

Edward III., Cast from Seals R. xi. 7

Coin R. xxiii. 7

Seal R. xi. 7

Edward VI., Silver coin R. xxxiii. 7

First Prayer Book: MS. notes in copy at Beccles C. i. 67

Edward the Black Prince, Ring supposed to have belonged to C. iv. 181

Edwards, Dr John, Facsimile of writing C. iii. 119

Effigy of a Bishop in Trinity Church R. xl. xiii

Egyptian Antiquities R. xlvii. cx

bronze statuette R. xxxvi. 22

Fragment of a Graeco-Egypt. work on Magic 8vo Pub. No. ii.

Graeco-Egyptian papyrus in the British Museum C. i. 37

Sarcophagus of Ramses III. C. iii. 371, 383

skulls R. xlvii. cx: xlviii. cxxxvi

skulls, of xxvi. Dynasty Pr. vii. 17

skulls, Teeth of early R. xlvii. cx

stelae Pr. vii. 3: viii. 143

Stone implements from Helwan C. iv. 85

Egypt, A mummy's treasures recently discovered in the Delta C. iv. 385

The lake of Moeris and the Patriarch Joseph C. vi. 177

Eikon Basilike R. xlii. xxxvii

Election of Burgesses for the University R. xiv. 7; xx. 7

Elingheims Church, Island of Gothland, Bronze Gothic thurible R. xl. xiv

Elizabeth, Queen, Canopy carried over, 1564 Pr. vii. 194

Correspondence with Henry IV. of France R. xxiv. 7

Elmham, Plaque R. xlvii. xcviii, c.

Elsworth Church, Work in progress at Pr. viii. 28

Ely, Bronze sword from the river R. xlvii. xcviii

Description of the Sextry Barn, by R. Willis. 4 plates 4to Pub. No. vii

Roman coin R. xiv. 6

Roman pottery R. xli. xxv

Romano-British remains R. xli. xxv

Token "W. Gotobed 1662" R. xliv. cvii

Ely Cathedral, Chapter house
Pr. viii. 242

Ely, Episcopal Visitation of the Archdeaconry, 1685 C. iii. 323

Formation of the Diocese
Pr. vii. 157

Liber Archidiaconi Eliensis
R. xxxiii. 7

Mortuary Roll sent forth by the
Prior and Convent, 1336-7
C. i. 125

Transcript of a Register of Property
of monastery R. xxxiii. 30

Purchase of the Manor and advowson
of Mepal in the xiv. century by
the Prior and Convent of
Pr. vii. 131

Ely, Isle of, British shields
4to Pub. No. xiv., part 2

Flint implements R. xxxvi. 9

Palstaves R. xxxvi. 9

See Downham Field, Littleport,
Mepal

Emmanuel College. See Cambridge

Enamelled plate, representing the Last
Judgement R. xx. 7

England, Visit of F. Burmann to, 1702
R. xxii. 8: xxv. 8

Engravers. G. M., a wandering Flemish artist, xv—xvi. century
C. iii. 247

Engraving on a reindeer's bone
R. xxxvi. 10

Engravings fastened into the Lambeth
copy of the Salisbury Primer or
Horae, printed by Wynkyn de
Worde, 1494 C. iii. 257

Copper, by G. M., xv.—xvi. century
C. iii. 247

Copper, fastened into the Cambridge
copy of the Utrecht Breviary of
1514 C. iii. 255

Copper, Calendars, 1477, believed to
be the earliest book with
R. xxvi. 8

Copper, Bible prints by R. Whitehall,
1677 R. xxxvii. xii

Engravings (continued)
Earliest English, of the Image of
Pity C. iii. 135

relating to the Stuarts
R. xlii. xxxvii

Wood, xv. century, pasted in a book
printed at Cologne, 1477
R. xxvi. 8

Enkhuizen, Ancient Library
Pr. viii. 359

Episcopal Church in Scotland, Documents connected with... in the
reign of Q. Anne C. ii. 225

Epitaph of M. Verrius Flaccus
C. vi. 313

Erasmus, St, Drawings of martyrdom
R. xlvii. 102

The Light of... and on the various
spellings of his name in the Trinity
Parish accounts C. iv. 327

Eros, Signet of C. v. 363

Essex, Jas., Journal of a tour through
part of Flanders and France, in
August, 1773, edited by W. M.
Fawcett. With portrait of Essex.
1888 8vo Pub. No. xxiv.

Tour in Flanders R. xlvi. lxx

MSS. in the British Museum
R. xvi. 10

Account of the old Chapel, Sidney
College R. xxxviii. xvi

Essex, Survey of Manors in the county
of Pr. vi. 17

See Arkesden, Ashdon, Chesterford,
Colchester, Newport, Great Hallingbury, Saffron Walden, Stratford

Eton, Frescoes in College Chapel
Pr. viii. 92

Etruscan Intaglio: The fall of Capaneus C. vi. 378

inscription at Perugia Pr. viii. 253

mirrors with engraved reverses
C. v. 185

Evangelia Augustini Gregoriana.
Edited by J. Goodwin. 1847
4to Pub. No. xiii.

Eversden, Gt., Roman millstone
R. xliii. lxxxiii
"Ewin, Thomas Cambridge, 1736"
Glass bottle with name R. xlv. vii
Exeter, Thos. Beaufort, Duke of, Let-
ter to the University, c. 1416
C. iii. 273
Exeter, Pavement in Exchequer Cham-
ber R. vii. 4
Exning, Roman coins R. xliii. lxxxvi
Expenses, School and College, in the
16th and 17th Centuries C. v. 201
Expositio hymnorum and Expositio
sequentiarum, 1502 R. xlvii. cii
Eye, Suffolk, Charter of the Monastery,
1137 R. xxvi. 8

Fahy Chapel, Ballycroy, Plans
R. xiv. 7
Fairs: Bury St Edmunds, Tract
R. xviii. 8
Garlic Fair Pr. viii. 313
Sturbridge, Tract R. xviii. 8
Falx, Bronze, found in the Fens
C. i. 361
Farndale, Bronze object R. xxxiii. 30
Faulder, W. W., Eight swords (1 plate).
1878 C. iv. 377
Faustina, Empress, Coin Pr. vii. 189
Fawcett, W. M., James Essex's Journal
of a Tour in Flanders and France,
1773. 1888 8vo Pub. No. xxiv.
Old glass with coats of arms, from
Waterbeach Church. 1871
R. xxxiii. 27
Antiquities found in digging the
foundations for the Museum of
Experimental Physics. 1872
R. xxxiii. 33
Coin, apparently of Hadrian. 1872
R. xxxiii. 33
La Pyrotechnie de Hanzelet Lorrain,
1630. 1873 R. xxxiii. 36
Gold chatelaine. 1874
R. xxxvi. 11
Bronze fibula, Roman, from Seaton,
Northants. 1875 R. xxxvi. 15

Fawcett, W. M. (continued)
The Basilica and Porta Nigra at
Trier. 1877. (3 plates)
R. xxxviii. xiii
Mainz Cathedral, change made in
the western dome. 1877
R. xxxviii. xiv
Tomb of Hildegarde. 1877
R. xxxviii. xiv
Minster Church at Aachen. 1882
R. xlii. xlix
Recent discoveries in Jesus College
Chapel. 1883 R. xliii. lxxxvi
on G. F. Browne's paper on Symbols
in Ledsham Church. 1886
R. xlvi. lxvii
Chained library at Zutphen. 1886
R. xlvi. lxix
Portions of a cinerary urn from
Nayland, Suffolk. 1887
R. xlvii. cv
Recent discoveries in Linton Church.
1889. (2 plates.) Pr. vii. 15
The family of Veysy. 1889
Pr. vii. 93
Death of the Rev. S. S. Lewis. 1891
Pr. vii. 288
Work in progress at Elsworth
Church, Cambs. 1891
Pr. viii. 28
Featherstone, J., Confirmation of Arms
to Alexander Amcottes. 1859
R. xix. 8
Autograph letter of Sir Wm. Dugdale.
1859 R. xix. 8
Document bearing the signatures
and seals of R. Dudley, Earl of
Leicester, and Wm. Cecil, Lord
Burleigh. 1859 R. xix. 8
Will of Sir John Hampden, 1457.
1859 R. xix. 8
Felmersham and Radwell, Receipts for
parsonage and glebe R. xxxiii. 19
Fen Ditton. See Ditton
Fen Road, The great, and its path to
the sea R. xv. 10; Pr. vii. 112
Fen Way R. xv. 10

Fens, British Falx   C. I. 361
Idolatry in the   R. xlvii. ciii
Fenstanton, Figure of Mercury, and
terra-cotta head   R. xl. xvi
Ferguson, R. S. Exhibition of squeeze
by E. C. Clark, from Roman In-
scription at Carlisle. 1892
Pr. viii. 85
Ferguson, John. John Francis Vigani,
first Professor of Chemistry in the
University. 1894   Pr. viii. 380
Fibula, Bronze, from Cambridge
R. xxv. 10
Bronze, from Diss   R. xliii. lxxxvi
Bronze, from Haslingfield
R. xxxvi. 27
from Burwell   R. xliv. cxxvii
Irish, from Ballycroy, co. Mayo
R. xxxiii. 27
Roman, from Seaton, Northants.
R. xxxvi. 15
Fibula-mould, Anglo-Saxon, from Lin-
coln   R. xli. xix
Fibulae, Anglo-Saxon from Hasling-
field   R. xxxvi. 11
Anglo-Saxon from Newnham
R. xiv. 7
from near Royston
R. xlviii. cxxxviii
from Landesborough Park
R. xliv. cxxix
Silver   R. xxxvi. 23
Figure, Alabaster, from Papworth
Everard   R. xl. xii
Brass, of an Ecclesiastic, from
Conington Church   R. xxxiii. 20
Bronze, from Kirkwell, Orkney
Islands   Pr. vii. 13
of a Saint from Guilden Morden
R. xlviii. cxl
Silver   R. xxxvi. 21
Figures, Ivory, mostly Flemish
R. xxxvi. 20
in the Antiquarian Museum
R. xlvii. c
Finch, Sir John, Arms at Padua
Pr. viii. 337

Fine Art as applied to the illustration
of the Bible   Pr. vii. 31
Fire-place in Master's Lodge, Christ's
College   C. vi. 374
Fisher, Bp, Papers   R. xxiv. 8
Funeral Sermon on Lady Margaret
R. xxxiii. 15
Fisher, Marshall, Terra-cotta vase
from Downham Field, Ely. 1882
R. xlii. xlvii
Fish-ponds, Manor House and Col-
lege, &c.   C. iii. 287
Fitzwilliam Museum. See Cambridge
Flaccus, Verrius, Epitaph   C. vi. 313
Flanders and France, Journal of a
tour through, 1773, by Jas. Essex
8vo Pub. No. xxiv.
Flaxman, John, Drawing R. xxxvii. x
Flemish artist of the xv—xvi. cen-
tury: G. M.   C. iii. 247
Ivory figures   R. xxxvi. 20
Palimpsest brasses   R. xii. 8
Flint 'cores,' or masses, from Ickling-
ham   R. xxiii. 8
flakes from Fen Ditton
R. xxxvi. 24
flakes from flint 'cores' or masses
R. xxiii. 8
trade at Brandon   R. xlv. xxxiii
Flint implements, Skull of Bos Primi-
genius associated with C. ii. 285
See Arrow-heads. Axe. Hammer.
Stone Implements
Flints from Carnac   R. xxxvi. 24
Worked, from Mildenhall
R. xxxix. xi
Wrought, from Grimes Graves
R. xxxvi. 26
Flintshire: Wat's Dyke
Florence, Medicean Library at
Pr. viii. 4
Floyer, M., Sickle from Trumpington.
1879   R. xl. xii
Foord, John, of Upton Cheyney, In-
ventory of goods, 1627 R. xxv. 8
Forceps found under King's Parade
R. xxxvi. 20

Fordham, F. N., Gold coins of James I.,
from Royston. 1881 R. xlii. xxxvii
Fordham, Chantry　　　　C. i. 211
Forged Curiosities　　　　R. xxxiii. 25
Forms of prayer at Coronations and
at the consecration of Peterhouse
Chapel　　　　　　　　R. xxiv. 8
Fortuna Nemesis, Silver statuette
C. v. 273
Foss Ditch, near Brandon　　C. i. 95
Foster, J. E., Diary of Alderman
Samuel Newton, 1662—1717.
1890　　　　8vo Pub. No. xxiii
Crown piece of George III. 1874
R. xxxvi. 15
Gold pattern crown piece of Q. Vic-
toria, 1848. 1874　R. xxxvi. 15
Pair of gloves said to have belonged
to Charles I. 1874　R. xxxvi. 15
Brocaded purses, temp. Charles I.
1874　　　　　　R. xxxvi. 15
A pincushion. 1874　R. xxxvi. 15
Five-guinea piece of William and
Mary. 1875　　　R. xxxvi. 15
Worked flints, from near Milden-
hall. 1878　　　　R. xxxix. xi
Roman Cinerary Urn. 1879
R. xxxix. xviii
Ground plan of the Studiola at
Pembroke College. 1879
R. xxxix. xviii
'La Maison Plantin' at Antwerp.
1879　　　　　　　C. iv. 271
On a vase exhibited by Mr Wilkin-
son. 1881　　　R. xlii. xxxvii
Portrait of Charles I. in the vestry
of St Michael's Church. 1881
R. xlii. xxxvii
Extracts from Alderman Newton's
Diary. 1886　　　R. xlvi. lxx
Two books printed by John Siberch.
1891　　　　　　　Pr. viii. 31
On A. Gray's Charters of St Rade-
gund's Priory. 1894 Pr. viii. 313
Foster, J. E. and T. D. Atkinson,
Catalogue of Loan Collection of
Plate, 1895. See Plate

Foster, W. K., Excavations of an
Anglo-Saxon Cemetery at Bar-
rington, Cambs. 1880. (12 plates
and 3 ill.)　　　　　C. v. 5
Bequest to the Society　Pr. viii. 56
Fountains Abbey, Inscription on Tablet
on a Corn Mill　　R. xxxiii. 20
Fox, Buscall (of Barton Mills), A
terracotta vase and a Roman coin
from West Row Fen, Mildenhall.
1882　　　　　　　R. xlii. lxxi
Foxton, Offa's bridge and Offa's brook
R. xli. xiv
Roman pottery　R. xii. 7; C. i. 43
Saxon beads　　　　R. xxxvi. 26
France and Flanders, Journal of Tour
through, 1773, by Jas. Essex
8vo Pub. No. xxiv
Activity of volcanoes of central
R. xxv. 7
Coins R. xxxiii. 31, 36; xxxviii. xi
Gallic Staters　　　R. xxxvi. 10
See St Acheul. Amiens. Carnac.
Citeaux. Clairveaux. Dordogne.
La Madelaine. Tours.
Franciscans at Douay　R. xxi. 9
Franks, Sir A. W., Palimpsest sepul-
chral Brasses. 1848. 1 plate
4to Pub. No. xiv. part 1
Genealogical history of the Freville
family; with some account of the
monuments in Little Shelford
Church. 1848. 3 plates
4to Pub. No. xiv. part 4
Pavement of encaustic tiles. 1848
R. ix. 6
Account of the family of Freville.
1848　　　　　　　R. viii. 7
Deed granting arms to King's Col-
lege. 1848　　　　R. ix. 6
Medieval Seals formed out of Roman
Intaglios. 1849　　R. x. 5
Casts from seals of Edward III.
1850　　　　　　　R. xi. 7
Frederick, Crown Prince of Germany,
Medal commemorating his mar-
riage　　　　　R. xliv. cxxiv

Free Chapels and Chantries, Notes on
C. I. 201
Fresco at Buckenham   R. xlvii. cii
in Chesterton Church   C. iv. 3
Frescoes in Eton College Chapel
Pr. viii. 92
in Stoke Church, Suffolk   R. ix. 8
of St George and the Dragon in
Pickering Church   Pr. vii. 131
See also *Paintings*
Freville Family, Genealogical history
4to Pub. No. xiv. part 4
Fulbourn, Chantry   C. i. 211
Roman excavations   C. iii. 313
Sculptured Stone   Pr. vii. 17
S. Vigor's Church, enlarged and
restored   C. iii. 215
Furniture of the old Provost's Lodge
of King's College   C. iv. 223

Gadow, H., Early Christian Inscription
from Mertola, Portugal; with
remarks by E. C. Clark. 1888
Pr. vii. 7
Galatius   Episcopus   Sarsinatensis,
Seal   R. xvii. 9
Gallic coins   R. xxxiii. 35; xxxvi. 10;
Pr. vii. 135
remains   R. xl. xvi
staters in France   R. xxxvi. 10
Gallienus, Coins.   See *Coins*, Roman
Garlic Fair and Garlic Row
Pr. viii. 313
Garnet, Almandine, set in gold
R. xxxvi. 17
' Garret,' Origin of the word
R. xlii. xlix
Garway, Herefordshire, Arch   R. x. 6
Gasquet, F. A., On W. H. Shimield's
paper on Shengay. 1890
Pr. vii. 146
Gem, Almandine Garnet   R. xxxvi. 17
Antique Intaglio Sard, probably 3rd
century   R. xxxviii. ix
Christian engraved, in the Lewis
collection   Pr. vii. 171
Etruscan Intaglio   C. vi. 378

Gem (*continued*)
Inscribed, from Dublin R. xxxiii. 17
Red jaspar intaglio from Smyrna
R. xliv. cxxxvi
Head of Livia, from a   R. xxxiii. 36
Gems, Four Gnostic, added to the
Lewis collection   C. vi. 347
Two intaglio, a sard and an ame-
thyst   R. xxxvi. 15
Two remarkable engraved, of early
Christian work   C. v. 1
Gem-types, Two unpublished Chris-
tian   C. v. 75
George, St, Anglo-Saxon Notices
R. x. 10
George, St, of Cappadocia, Cultus
Pr. vii. 147
Syriac and Coptic versions of the
martyrdom   Pr. vii. 133
George, St, and the Dragon, Frescoes
of, in Pickering Church
Pr. vii. 131
George III., coin   R. xxxvi. 15
Gerard, John, Letters   C. iv. 7
German coins   R. xxvi. 8; xxxiii. 37
Germany, Roman wall in South
R. xlii. xlvi
See *Aachen. Brunswick. Moringen.*
Gibson, E. W., Two mother-of-pearl
beads from Great Shelford. 1885
R. xlvi. lx
Gibson, G. S., of Saffron Walden,
Ancient Cemetery in grounds of
R. xxxvi. 24
Gibson, John, Letters   Pr. viii. 64
Giles, John (of Caxton), Mill-stones
from Caldecote and Caxton. 1884
R. xliv. cxxxvii
Girton, Anglo-Saxon remains
R. xlvi. lxxiv
Chantry   C. i. 211
Cinerary Urns   Pr. viii. 282
Deed relating, xvii. century
R. xxxiii. 21
Roman and Saxon cemetery
R. xli. xx.; xlii. 1
See *How House*

Glamorganshire. See *Castell*
Glass from Waterbeach Church
R. xxxiii. 27
in windows of the Library of St
Alban's Abbey Pr. viii. 213
See also *Bottle*
Glossaries, Mediaeval, Study of
R. xliv. cxxv
Gloucester, Eleanor Cobham, Duchess
of, Lament C. i. 177
Gloucestershire. See *Deerhurst.*
Tewkesbury
Glover, John, An uncial ms. of St
Mark's gospel, ix. century. 1862
R. xxii. 6
Gloves of Charles I. R. xxxvi. 15
Goche, Dr Barnaby, Election as
Burgess in Parliament
C. iii. 203
Godwin's Catalogue of Bishops, 1615.
Annotated copy R. xxv. 8
Gold Chatelaine R. xxxvi. 11
Goldsmith, Oliver, "The Three
Pigeons," near Thame, Oxon.,
probably the scene of 'She Stoops
to Conquer' R. xliii. lxxi
Gonville and Caius College. See *Cambridge*
Goodman, Godfrey, Letter and materials for life C. ii. 113: R. xx. 7
Goodman, Neville, Burial urns found
near the mouth of the Amazon
River. 1880. (18 ill.) C. iv. 411
Goodwin, C. W., Two British Shields
found in the Isle of Ely (4 plates).
1848 4to Pub. xiv., No. 2
Anglo-Saxon legends of St Andrew
and St Veronica. 1851
8vo Pub. No. i
Fragment of a Graeco-Egyptian
work upon Magic (1 plate). 1852
8vo. Pub. No. ii
Legendary adventures of St Andrew. 1848 R. ix. 5
Abstract of an account of the Anglo-
Saxon legend of St Veronica.
1850 C. i. 3; R. xi. 7

Goodwin, C. W. (*continued*)
Graeco-Egyptian **papyrus** in the
British Museum. 1851 C. i. 37
Two fragments of the Acts of the
Martyrs Chamoul and Justus, in
the Sahidic dialect, on a **papyrus**
in the British Museum. 1855
C. i. 71
Goodwin, J., Account of the rites and
ceremonies which took place at
the Consecration of Archbishop
Parker, with notes (1 plate). 1841
4to Pub. No. iii
Evangelia Augustini Gregoriana.
A description of mss. 286 and 197
in the Parker Library (11 plates).
1847 4to Pub. No. xiii
Gothland, Island of, Thurible
R. xl. xiv
'Gotobed, Wm., 1622,' Ely token
R. xliv. cvii
Gotz, Nicolaus, Book printed by, at
Cologne, 1477 C. iii. 244
Device, &c. C. iii. 237
Graeco-Buddhistic fragments from the
Peshawur Valley Pr. viii. 142
Graeco-Egyptian papyrus in the British
Museum C. i. 37
work on Magic, Fragments
8vo Pub. No. ii
Grain-rubbers from Anglesea Abbey
and Mildenhall R. xxi. 8
Gransden, Gt., Curiosities
R. xxxiii. 21
Grantchester, Moat and Hall
C. iii. 287
Church, Recent discoveries
C. iv. 63
Gratianus, Coins. See *Coins:* Roman
Gravel Hill Farm, Huntingdon Road,
Glass bottles C. ii. 289
Roman interments R. xxi. 8
Gray, Arthur, Some xii. century Charters of the Priory of St Radegund,
Cambridge. 1894 Pr. viii. 304
Gray, Thos., House in which he was
born R. xxiii. 7

Greece, Archaeological Studies in
R. xxii. 7

Greek Imperial coin found in Cambridge C. ii. 1

Green, O., Portions of a Roman Situla from Gt. Chesterford. 1870
R. xxxiii. 24

Green, W. Wiles, Exhibited fragments of rough pottery. 1888
Pr. vii. 2

Collection of Antiquities from Manea. 1892 Pr. viii. 87

Greenstone implement from the Cave of Le Moustier, Dordogne
R. xxxviii. xix

Gregory the Great. Evangelia Augustini Gregoriana, ed. J. Goodwin. 1847. 4to Pub., No. xiii

Griffith, A. F., Flint implement found at Barnwell. 1878 (2 plates)
C. iv. 177

Flint implement from near Horningsey. 1878 R. xxxix. xi

Romano-British Urns from near the Observatory. 1878
R. xxxix. xi

Palaeolithic flint implement, probably from the Chesterton gravel pits. 1879 R. xl. xiii

Two Urns from Peru. 1880
R. xl. xxvii

Perforated pebble and two worked deer tynes from Ditton. 1880
R. xl. xxvii

Objects found in the Anglo-Saxon cemetery at Barrington. 1880
R. xli. xii

Pottery rings from Harston and Barrington. 1882 R. xlii. li

Griffith, Wm., Notes on Charib implements in Barbadoes, and the neighbouring (West Indian) Islands. 1873 C. iii. 295

Flint arrow-head from Upper Canada. 1873 R. xxxvi. 9

Stone axe from Lake Superior. 1873 R. xxxvi. 9

Griffith, Wm. (continued)
Flint implements and pottery found at Cissbury, near Worthing. 1874
R. xxxvi. 10

Letter from G. H. Hawtayne, on the origin and usages of the Charibs. 1874 R. xxxvi. 11

Grimes Graves, near Thetford, Flint implements R. xxxiii. 16

Worked flints R. xxxvi. 26

Grosseto, Statuette from R. xxxvi. 22

Grove, W. R., Romano-British cinerary vase from Haddenham Fen. 1879 R. xl. xii

Bronze figure of Mercury from near Fenstanton. 1880 R. xl. xvi

Terra-cotta head from Fenstanton. 1880 R. xl. xvi

de Gruey, W., Land measures employed in the Channel Islands. 1886
C. vi. 305

Guest, E., Offa's Dyke from the parish of Mold to the sea. 1858
R. xviii. 9

Activity of the volcanoes of Central France since the Christian Era. 1864 R. xxv. 7

Guilden Morden, Figure
R. xlviii. cxl

Inscribed vase C. iv. 337

Guildford, Chained library Pr. viii. 1

Guy of Warwick, French version
R. xlvii. cvii

Gwynne, Dr, Letter from R. Booth
C. ii. 139

Letter from Dr Goodman R. xx. 7

Haddenham Fen, Romano-British vase R. xl. xii

Haddiscoe, Inscription in St Mary's Church R. xl. xxiv

Haddon, A. C., Ethnology and Archaeology of the Aran Islands, county Galway. 1894 Pr. viii. 358

Hadrianus, Coins. See Coins: Roman

Hadrian's Wall R. xlii. 43

Hague, Dutch Records at the R. xxv. 9
Relics of Barentz   R. xxxvii. xi
Hailstone, Edward, *Junr.*, History
and Antiquities of the Parish of
Bottisham, and of the Priory of
Anglesey (7 Plates), and Supple-
ment. 1873–8
8vo Pub. Nos. xiv. xvi
Ring found at Montpensier, sup-
posed to have belonged to the
Black Prince.   1878 (Illustra-
tions in text.)   C. iv. 181
Seal representing St Lawrence, found
in Bottisham Fen. 1870
R. xxxiii. 20
Hall, John, of Kipping, MS. Books
R. xlvi. lxviii
Hallingbury, Gt., Holes for cooking
R. xxxvi. 11
Halliwell[-Phillips], J. O., Catalogue
of Books given to Corpus Christi
College, by Thomas Markaunt,
1439, with their prices, 1848
4to Pub. xiv. No. 3
Suggestions towards the production
of an "Athenae Cantabrigienses."
1852   C. i. 49
Halse, Lid of Chest at   R. xvi. 10
Halton, Cross at   R. xlvii. 105
Hammer, Flint, found near Burwell
C. ii. 201
Stone, from Swaffham Fen.
R. xxxiii. 15
Hammers, Stone, Imitations
R. xvii. 10
Hammond, C. E., Presented a medie-
val bottle found at Newmarket.
1883.   R. xliii. lxxvii
Hamond's plan of Cambridge, 1572
Pr. vii. 13
Hampden, Sir John, Will, 1457
R. xix. 8
Hampden, John, Volume relating to
Trial   R. xviii. 8
Hardwick, C., St Catharine of Alex-
andria ; with a semi-Saxon legend.
(2 plates.) 1849 4to Pub. No. xv

Hardwick, C. (*continued*)
Specimens of the dialect of N.
Yorks. 1847   R. viii. 5
A satirical poem, *circa* 1320. 1848
R. ix. 6
Anglo-Saxon notices of St George.
1850   R. x. 10
Account of a very scarce "Lyfe of
St Rhadegunde." 1851 C. i. 29
Churches in Nurnburgh. 1852
R. xii. 7
The Jews' Synagogue at Prague.
1852   R. xii. 7
Impression of a seal. 1853
R. xiii. 6
"Articuli Universitatis Canta-
brigiae": a form of petition ad-
dressed to K. Henry V, about
1415, in vindication of some an-
cient usages, with notes. 1853
C. i. 85
MS. Life of K. Edward the Con-
fessor. 1854   R. xiv. 7
Lament of Eleanor Cobham, Duchess
of Gloucester, when convicted of
sorcery. 1854   C. i. 177
Foundation of St Catharine's Col-
lege. 1858   R. xviii. 8
Robert Woodlark, Founder and first
Master of St Catharine's Hall.
1858. (1 plate)   C. i. 329
Hardwick, Supposed antique from
R. viii. 6
Hare, Robert, Life   R. xxv. 9
Harpur, John, Psalter, xv. century,
written for   R. xxxviii. xvi
Harston, Pottery rings   R. xlii. li
Skulls   R. xlvii. cvii
Harthacnut, Coin   R. xxiii. 7
Harvey, Wm., Arms at Padua, *circa*
1598   Pr. viii. 337
Haslingfield, Anglo-Saxon fibulae and
beads   R. xxxvi. 20
Anglo-Saxon remains
R. xxxvi. 25 : xxxvii. xii
British jar   Pr. viii. 331
Chantry   C. i. 212

Haslingfield (continued)
Coin of Coenwulf   R. xxxvi. 25
Flint implement   R. xxvi. 17
Horse-bell   R. xxxix. 11
Iron sword   R. xxxvii. xiii
Miscellaneous objects   R. xxxix. 12
Remains   R. xxxvi. 23
Roman and Saxon remains
   R. xxxvi. 25
Romano-British pottery
   R. xxxvii. xii
Hauxton, Antiquities   Pr. vii. 24
Coins and other objects
   R. xlviii. cxxxvi
Painting of St Thomas of Canterbury, in Church   Pr. viii. 75
Roman Villa   R. xxxiii. 25
Hawk, Sore, Notice of a gift or render of a   C. i. 169
Hawksmoor, Nic., Letter to St John's College on proposed new bridge
   C. vii. 254
Hawtayne, C. H., Letter on the Charibs. 1858   R. xxxvi. 11
Haytian Coins   R. xxi. 6
Head, Terra-cotta, from Icklingham
   R. xliii. lxxii
Hebrew Coins. See Coins
Helwan, near Cairo, Flint implements
   C. iv. 85
Henry II., Coins
   R. xxiii. 7: xxxix. xii, xvi
Henry IV., of France, Correspondence with Q. Elizabeth
   R. xxiv. 7
Henry V., Articuli Univ. Cantab. A form of petition   C. i. 85
MS. Life, by R. Redmayne
   R. xxi. 8
Henry VI., Coin   R. xiii. 68
Henry VIII., Lamentation on death. Broadsheet   R. xx. 7
Process of legates in case of divorce of   R. xxiv. 7
Coin   R. xxxiii. 7
Henslow, J. S., Roman-British Remains. On the materials of two

Henslow, J. S. (continued)
sepulchral vessels found at Warden, Beds. (2 plates.) 1846
   4to Pub. No. xii
Presented flint implements from near Amiens. 1861.   R. xxii. 6
Heraldry, University and Collegiate, by H. A. Woodham. 2 parts. 1841-2   4to Pub., Nos. iv. and v
Armorial Ensigns of the University and Colleges, and of the Regius Professors   Pr. viii. 107
Arms granted to Alex. Amcottes, 1549   R. xix. 9
Arms granted to King's College
   R. ix. 6
Arms of Arundel, Bishop of Ely, in Landbeach Church
   C. iv. 255
Sir Thos. Baines, at Padua
   Pr. viii. 344
De L'Isle, Bishop of Ely, in Landbeach Church   C. iv. 255
Sir John Finch, at Padua
   Pr. viii. 344
Guild of Corpus Christi, in Landbeach Church   C. iv. 255
Wm. Harvey, at Padua
   Pr. viii. 344
Millington   C. i. 338
Richard Willoughby at Padua
   Pr. viii. 344
Woodlarke   C. i. 338
on old glass from Waterbeach Church   R. xxxiii. 27
Heralds' Visitations of the County of Cambridge   C. ii. 67
Hereford Cathedral, Chained Library
   Pr. viii. 1
Herefordshire, Survey of Manors
   Pr. vi. 17
See Garway. Kilpeck. Rollestone
Hertfordshire. See Anstey. Brent Pelham. Hitchin. Pelham Furneaux. Radwell
Hessels, J. H., The study of Medieval Glossaries. 1884   R. xliv. cxxv

Hewett, Mr (afterwards Rev. J. W.),
Rubbings of brasses. 1848
R. ix. 6
Heysham, Cross R. xlvii. cv
Hickson, S. J. 'Sakit' Canoes. 1891.
Illustrations in text R. vii. 289
Hildegarde, Tomb R. xxxviii. 14
Hill-forts of N. Wales R. xli. xvii
Histon, Chantry C. i. 213
Hitchin, British coins Pr. vii. 152
Hobblers from Barnwell
R. xxxiii. 27
Hobson, Thos., Deed to Thomas New-
man R. xxii. 8
House, 'the White Horse,' and the
late Mr Cory's house C. iii. 405
Hodgetts, J. F., 'Smith' and 'Wright'
in Anglo-Saxon times. 1886
R. xlvii. xciv
'Hoisting' by an earthquake
R. xxxvii. x
Holinshed, Table of distances between
different towns in his description
of England C. iv. 259
Holland, Letter to the Earl of, 1641
R. xi. 8
Holland. See Dutch. Zutphen
Homer, Portrait on coin of Nicaea
C. v. 41
Hood, David, of Cambridge, Medal,
1796, by: and information con-
cerning R. xxxiii. 8
Hooppell, Dr, Stone implements, bronze
celt and medieval jug from near
Littleport. 1880 R. xli. xiv
Stone-grinder from Vinovium. 1880
R. xli. xv
The Roman station of Binchester.
1880 R. xlii. xli
Hope, W. H. St John, Armorial En-
signs of the University and Col-
leges, and of the Regius Pro-
fessors. 1892. (32 ill.)
Pr. viii. 107
Cluniac Priory at Castle Acre, Nor-
folk. 1893 Pr. viii. 243
Horne. See Primer

Horham Hall, Architectural History
Pr. vii. 210
Horningsey, History of, by W. K.
Clay. 1865 8vo Pub. No. vii
History of R. xlv. xxxii
Bronze axe R. xxxvi. 22
Celt R. xxi. 6
Coins R. xxii. 6
Spoon bowl R. xlvi. lx
Stone implement R. xxxix. xi
Horse-bell from Haslingfield
R. xxxix. xi
Ireland R. xxxix. xix
Horse-bells from neighbourhood of
Cambridge R. xxxix. xvii
used for business purposes
R. xxxix. xix
Horse-shoes, Saxon, from Barrington
R. xxxix. xix
Roman, from Cambridge
R. xli. xxv
Roman, from Caxton
R. xliii. lxxxiii
from Stuntney Fen R. xlvi. lxxi
Hostels, Early University Statutes
concerning C. ii. 279
Hotham, John de, Bishop of Ely,
Mortuary Roll C. i. 125
Hours, Illustrated MS book of, French
R. xxxvi. 25
How House, Girton, Ancient Chapel
near Pr. viii. 55
Roman interments R. xxi. 8
Howard, F. G., Recent discoveries in
Grantchester Church. 1877
C. iv. 63 : R. xxxvii 14
von Hügel, Baron A., Antiquities
found with Saxon skeletons at
Girton. 1886. R. xlvi. lxxiv
Exhibits recent accessions to the
Museum
R. xlvii. xcviii : Pr. vii. 294 :
viii. 31
Canoe, weapons and stone imple-
ments from the Islands of the
Pacific, Australia, &c. 1887
R. xlviii. cxxxiv

von Hügel, Baron A. (continued)
Roman refuse pit in Alderney. 1890
Pr. vii. 175
Exhibits stone and bronze imple-
ments in the Foster bequest. 1892
Pr. viii. 56
Ancient well at Mountsorrel. 1892.
(1 plate and 1 ill.) Pr. viii. 133
on T. McK. Hughes's paper on An-
cient Ditches, &c. 1893
Pr. viii. 282
Urns found in Saxon burial-places
at St John's College and Girton.
1893 Pr. viii. 282
On C. L. Acland's paper on Antiqui-
ties of the immediate past. 1894
Pr. viii. 317
von Hügel, Baron A. and F. J. H.
Jenkinson, Saxon cemetery near
St John's College. 1888
R. xlviii. cxl
von Hügel, Baron A. and T. McK.
Hughes, Contents of a Roman
rubbish-hole at Great Chesterford.
1884 R. xlv. xii
Hughes, T. McK., Ivory knife-handle
found in the Thames. 1876
R. xxxvi. 21
Amphora found at Haslingfield.
1876 R. xxxvi. 23
Spindle-wheel from Haslingfield.
1876 R. xxxvi. 23
Bronze fibula from Haslingfield.
1876 R. xxxvi. 23
Bronze and stone (neolithic) imple-
ments from Brittany. 1876
R. xxxvi. 24
Pieces of flint and chalcedony from
Carnac. 1876 R. xxxvi. 24
Quartzite implements from Bois du
Rocher, Ganterie, Dinan. 1876
R. xxxvi. 24
Flint implements from St Acheul.
1876 R. xxxvi. 24
Coin of Coenwulf, King of Mercia,
from Haslingfield. 1876
R. xxxvi. 25

Hughes, T. McK. (continued)
An illustrated MS Book of Hours,
French. 1876 R. xxvi. 25
Three tumuli at Upper Hare Park.
1876 R. xxxvi. 26
Mode of formation of natural mounds
resembling tumuli. 1876
R. xxxvi. 26
Remains discovered at Cissbury.
1876 R. xxxvi. 26
Wrought flints from Grimes Graves.
1876 R. xxxvi. 26
Vase found near Chesterford. 1877
R. xxxvii. xiii
Intaglio sard in a silver setting.
1877 R. xxxviii. ix
On a carreg-lab. 1877
R. xxxviii. xii
Stone weapons in the Woodwardian
Museum. 1877 R. xxxviii. xii
Lleithvaen, a cure for Hydrophobia.
1877 R. xxxviii. xii
Greenstone implement from the
Cave of Le Moustier, Dordogne.
1877 R. xxxviii. xix
Flint implements from the Cave of
La Madelaine. 1878
R. xxxviii. xix
Bronze Celts from Tours. 1878
R. xxxviii. xix
Coin of Probus found near the Ob-
servatory. 1878 R. xxxviii. xix
Earthenware vessel, glass bead, and
bronze objects from Haslingfield.
1878 R. xxxix. xii
English Coins of Henry II., and
James II. 1878 R. xxxix. xii
On a Canoe imbedded in peat. 1878
R. xxxix. xii
Leaden vessels in the Library of
Trinity College, and at Westley
Waterless. 1879. 1 plate
R. xxxix. xiv
Coin and miscellaneous objects from
St Asaph. 1879 R. xxxix. xvi
Seal or secretum from Abergele.
1879 R. xxxix. xvi

Hughes, T. M^cK. (*continued*)
Stations of the neolithic age. 1879
                                R. xxxix. xvi
Roman kiln at Great Chesterford.
1879   R. xxxix. xvii
Horse-bells. 1879   R. xxxix. xvii
Cinerary urn from Trumpington.
1879   R. xxxix. xvii
Saxon horse-shoe from Barrington
and miscellaneous objects. 1879
                                R. xxxix. xviii
Manufacture of pottery in the Py-
renees. 1880   R. xl. xxvi
Roman remains from Wales. 1880
                                R. xli. xi
Token found in Trinity Hall. 1880
                                R. xli. xii
Wat's and Offa's Dykes. 1880
                                R. xli. xiii
Felstone implements from the valley
of the Elwy, N. Wales. 1881
                                R. xli. xvii
Ancient tribes and hill-forts of N.
Wales. 1881   R. xli. xvii
Bronze helmeted bust from the
Banks collection. 1881
                                R. xlii. xxxv
On remains found under two elms in
the grounds of St John's College,
and on rings of annual growth of
trees. 1881   R. xlii. xxxix
On Dr Hooppel's Explorations at
Binchester. 1881   R. xlii. xlii
On Roman pottery and other ob-
jects, exhibited by W. W. Cor-
deaux, Esq. 1882   R. xlii. xlvii
Archaeological notes on the neigh-
bourhood of Mentone. 1883
                                R. xliii. lxxix
On H. Middleton's paper on the
Legend of Atlantis. 1883
                                R. xliii. lxxxviii
On A. P. Maudslay's Explorations
in Central America. 1883
                                R. xliv. cxx
The Via Devana and Castle Hill.
1884   R. xliv. cxxxii

Hughes, T. M^cK. (*continued*)
Opening of a tumulus at Upper
Hare Park. 1884   R. xlv. ix
Bos longifrons. 1884   R. xlv. xi
Supposed Roman Camp at Whitley,
near Alston, and the Maiden Way
as a Roman Road. 1884
                                C. vi. 41
Three sepulchral mounds near Cros-
by Ravensworth, Westmoreland.
1884   R. xlv. xii
Medieval Earthenware pig, glass
bottle, metal mortars and pilgrim's
bottle found in digging the foun-
dations of the new Post Office.
1884   R. xlv. xiii
On B. Walker's paper on Ancient
Camps in Wiltshire. 1884
                                R. xlv. xvi
Results of excavations in the neigh-
bourhood of Newmarket. 1885
                                R. xlv. xxi
History of Horningsey. 1885
                                R. xlv. xxxii
Traces of a Roman village near
Shepreth. 1885   R. xlvi. lx
Objects recently acquired by the
Museum. 1887   R. xlvii. cxiii
Three mortars. 1887
                                R. xlviii. cxxxiii
Ancient earth-works between the
mouth of the Tyne and the Sol-
way (1 plate). 1887 C. vi. 355:
with remarks   R. xlviii. cxxxiv
On Limblow Hill, near Royston,
Cambs. 1888   C. vi. 395
Bronze figure found near Kirkwall,
Orkney Islands. 1889 Pr. vii. 13
Antiquities found near Hauxton.
1889. 3 plates   Pr. vii. 24
Presidential Address. 1889, 1891
                                Pr. vii. 86, 296
Gold reliquary from Rio Janeiro, &c.
1890   Pr. vii. 131
Stakes and pottery from a Wattle-
hut, Loch Maree. 1890
                                Pr. vii. 185

Hughes, T. M^cK. (*continued*)
Antiquities found at Great Thurlow. 1891   Pr. vii. 252
Death of the Rev. S. S. Lewis. 1891   Pr. vii. 286
Objects from ancient Indian cave-dwellings and cliff-dwellings in Arizona. 1891   Pr. viii. 23
Ancient ditches between Hobson street and Sidney street. (10 plates and 2 ill.) 1892–3   Pr. viii. 32, 256
Camp at Ardoch, Perthshire. 1892   Pr. viii. 57
Finds in Cambridge during the past year. 1892   Pr. viii. 74
On Mr W. Wiles Green's Collection of Antiquities found at or near Manea. 1892   Pr. viii. 87
Castle Hill, Cambridge. 1893 (2 plans and 5 ill.)   Pr. viii. 173
On T. C. Allbutt's paper on Trade in Amber. 1893   Pr. viii. 244
Ancient ditches and medieval remains near the Pitt Press. 1893 (2 plates and 2 ill.)   Pr. viii. 255
A small square piece of wood found in the ruins of Castell-y-Mynach, Glamorganshire. 1893   Pr. viii. 93
Crystal bowl, representing a Wyvern. 1894   Pr. viii. 390
A Universal Ring Dial, 'Henry Sutton fecit 1660.' 1894   Pr. viii. 392
Hughes, T. M^cK. and T. D. Atkinson, Roman House at Swaffham Prior. 1892   Pr. viii. 173, 229
Hughes, T. M^cK. and Baron A. von Hügel, Contents of a Roman rubbish-hole at Great Chesterford. 1884   R. xlv. xii
Hughes, T. M^cK. and F. J. H. Jenkinson, Preliminary report on excavations at Great Chesterford. 1880   R. xl. xvi

Hughes, T. M^cK. and F. J. H. Jenkinson (*continued*)
Further excavations. (1 plate.) 1880 R. xl. xxiv: Remarks by W. White   R. xl. xxvii
Results of investigations during excavations in Trinity Hall. 1880   R. xl. xxi
Hughes, T. M^cK. and A. Macalister, A newly discovered Dyke at Cherryhinton. 1894 Pr. viii. 317
Hughes, T. M^cK. and J. E. Marr, Flint flakes from Fen Ditton. 1876   R. xxxvi. 24
Roman and other remains from Fen Ditton. 1876   R. xxxvi. 24
Remains, from black-earth pits near Cambridge. 1876   R. xxxvi. 25
Roman vessels and Saxon spearhead from Haslingfield. 1876   R. xxxvi. 25
Hughes, Mrs T. M^cK., Ring-Dial from Cumberland. 1890 Pr. vii. 130
Frescoes of St George and the Dragon, in Pickering Church. 1890   Pr. vii. 131
Humphry, A. P., Bible prints by Robert Whitehall, 1677. 1877   R. xxxvii. xii
Iron sword from Haslingfield. 1897   R. xxxvii. xiii
Maces of the Esquire Bedells, and the Yeoman Bedell. 1879. 1 folding plate   C. iv. 207
The preservation of Maces. 1879.   R. xxxix. xiv
On R. Bowes' paper on the University Printers. 1884   R. xliv. cxxii
Humphry, Sir G. M., On human bones found at Burwell. 1884   R. xliv. cxxviii
On T. M^cK. Hughes and A. Macalister's paper on a Dyke. 1894   Pr. viii. 322
Hundred Rolls, Some terms used in the   C. vi. 65

Hunsbury, Triangular brick from
    R. xlvi. lxxiv
Hunstanton, Roman graves at
    C. iv. 423
Huntingdonshire, Survey of Manors
    Pr. vi. 17
See *Brampton. Earith. Fenstanton.
Gransden. Offord.*
Hurrell, Swann, Horse-bells. 1879
    R. xxxix. xix
A flat brass weight. 1879
    R. xxxix. xix
Offa's bridge near Foxton, and Offa's
    brook. 1880   R. xli. xiv
Bronze ring, a Roman bronze coin
    of the iv. century, &c., found at
    Newton. 1890   Pr. vii. 185
Hydrophobia, Grass at Lleithvaen a
    cure for   R. xxxviii. xii

Iceland, Studs of medieval belt
    R. xli. xiv
Littera Fraternitatis Concessa Wyt-
    frido Juarii Filio de Insula de
    Ysland   C. iv. 401
Ickleton, Foundations of buildings
    R. ix. 7
Icklingham, Flint 'cores' or masses
    R. xxiii. 8
Celt   R. xlii. xlii
Terra-cotta head   R. xliii. lxxii
Idolatry in the Fens   R. xlvii. ciii
'Image of Pity,' Earliest English en-
    gravings of   C. iii. 135
Implement, Bone, from Huntingdon
    Road   R. xxxiii. 13
Charib, from Barbadoes   C. iii. 295
Shell, from Barbadoes   R. xxxvi. 22
Implements of Antlers of red Deer
    R. xxiii. 19
of Stag's-horn
    R. xxxiii. 19; xl. xxvii
See also *Bronze, Fellstone, Flint,
Stone*
Indian Cave dwellings and cliff dwell-
    ings of Arizona   Pr. viii. 23
Indian Coin, 1833   R. xxxiii. 35

Indulgence known as the 'Image of
    Pity,' Earliest English engravings
    of   C. iii. 135
printed in Germany, 1489
    R. xxxvii. 9
of Dr Thomas Lane   R. xx. 7
Ingulf's History of Croyland Abbey
    Pr. vii. 207
Ingulf and the Historia Croylandensia
    by W. G. Searle 8vo. Pub. xxvii.
Inquisitio Comitatis Cantabrigiensis
    C. vi. 45; R. xlv. ix
Inscription, Athenian   R. xvii. 9
    containing name of Amasis
    R. xlvi. lxlii
Cuneiform, from Nineveh
    R. xliii. lxxxiii
Dutch, in Haddiscoe Church
    R. xl. xxiv
Early Christian, at Mertola, Portu-
    gal   R. vii. 7
Etruscan, at Perugia   Pr. viii. 253
in Lady Chapel at Peterborough
    R. xxxiii. 31
Keltiberian, at Saguntum
    R. xli. xxiii
Ogam, on sculptured stone
    Pr. vii. 88
on a bell   R. xxxiii. 15
on a vase   R. xxvi. 7
on clay, from Thebes   R. xlv. xxxix
on corn-mill near Fountains Abbey
    R. xxxiii. 20
on stone at Brough-under-Stanmore
    R. xlv. xxiii
Roman, at Carlisle   Pr. viii. 85
    at Thornhill   R. xlv. cxxxiv
near Huntingdon Road
    R. xiii. 7
on a slab of Parian Marble, in
    Trinity College Library
    C. vi. 313
Runic, on sculptured stone
    Pr. vii. 86
Inscriptions, Roman, on Huntingdon
    Road   R. xiii. 7
in Crete   R. xxiii. 8

Inscriptions (*continued*)
Spanish, from Mertola and Arizona
R. xlvii. cviii
On various, and supposed Inscriptions
C. vi. 1
Intaglio. See *Gem*
Inventory of goods of J. Foord, 1627
R. xxv. 8
Ireland, Horse-bell B. xxxix. xix
See *Aran. Ballycroy. Kildare. Lough Glyn*
Irish Coinage, Suggestions to Henry VIII. for an, by N. Tycry. Edited by G. O. White-Cooper and F. J. H. Jenkinson. 1886
8vo. Pub. No. xxii
Iselham, Chantry C. i. 213
Italian Casket, xv. century
R. xlvi. lxii
primer or touch-box R. xxxix. xix
Italy. See *Bologna. Canosa. Grosseto. Mantua. Orvieto. Scurgola*
Ivory figures, mostly Flemish
R. xxxv. 20
plaque from Elmham
R. xlvii. xcviii

Jackson, B. Daydon, Draft of a letter by John Gerard, with notes. 1876
C. iv. 7
Jaellinge, The Stone of Pr. vii. 18
James I., Visits to Newmarket
C. ii. 295
Coins R. xlii. xxxvii; xlv. ix
James II., Coins
R. xxxiii. 11; xxxix. xii
Letter of Christopher Rogerson concerning Christening of, 1639
R. xviii. 8
James, M. R., The Abbey of St Edmund at Bury. I. The Library, II. The Church. 1895. 1 plate.
8vo. Pub. No. xxviii
Sculpture at Amiens Cathedral. 1888 R. xlviii. cxxxix
Fine Art as applied to the illustration of the Bible, exemplified

James, M. R. (*continued*)
chiefly by Cambridge MSS. 1889 (8 plates) Pr. vii. 31, 76
Appendix: Verses from the Cloister Windows of St Alban's Abbey Pr. vii. 64
Frescoes in Eton College Chapel. 1892 Pr. viii. 92
Appendix: paintings at Eton and Winchester Pr. viii. 100
MS. Psalter in the University Library. 1892 Pr. viii. 146
Greek Psalter in the Library of Emmanuel College. (2 illus.) 1892 Pr. viii. 168
Glass in the windows of the Library of St Alban's Abbey. 1893
Pr. viii. 213
MS. of the New Testament in Latin in Pembroke College Library. 1893 Pr. viii. 221
Japanese coins R. xxxiii. 16, 36
Jar, British, from Haslingfield
Pr. viii. 331
Roman, from Burwell Fen
R. xxxiii. 15
Jasper, probably xiii. century
R. xxxvi. 20
Javelin, Reproduction of R. xxxiii. 36
Jegon, John, Bp of Norwich, Case of Wm. Sayer in Consistory Court of, c. 1612 R. xxi. 8
Jenkinson, F. J. H. British coins. 1880 R. xl. xxvii
Roman and Saxon Cemetery at Girton. 1881 R. xli. xx: xli. l
Roman rings and pottery from Chesterford (2 illus.) 1882
R. xlii. liv
The earliest account of the Mantuan vase. 1883 R. xliii. lxxvii
Exhibits a volume containing Expositio hymnorum and Expositio sequentiarum, printed by W. de Worde, 1502. 1886 R. xlvii. cii
Roman coins from Willingham, 1883
C. v. 225

Jenkinson, F. J. H. (*continued*)
MS. copy of the Scala of Johannes
Climacus, 1473. 1889 Pr. vii. 17
Book printed at Cambridge by John
Siberch. (1 illus.) 1889
Pr. vii. 104
Letter from P. Kaetz to J. Siberch,
printer at Cambridge. 1890
Pr. vii. 186
On A. Gray's paper on xiii. century
charters. 1894 Pr. viii. 313
On C. L. Acland's paper on Anti-
quities of the immediate past.
1894 Pr. viii. 317
and Baron A. von Hügel. See
Hügel
and T. M⁸K. Hughes. See *Hughes*
Jenkinson, F. J. H. and G. O. White-
Cooper, Tyery's Irish Coinage
(plates). 1888 8vo. Pub. No. xxii
Jerusalem, Marble lion at R. xxv. 8
Jesus College. See *Cambridge*
Jews' Synagogue at Prague R. xii. 7
Jodrell, Miss, Exhibits a medal of
Q. Anne, 1704. 1889 Pr. vii. 9
John, St, the Baptist, Representation
of his death, from Amiens Cathe-
dral R. xlviii. cxxxix
Brass signet with head of
R. xxxvi. 16
Johnson, Dr Jas. Legacy to Sidney
College R. xxiii. 9
Johnson, O. Pewter spoon-bowl from
Horningsey, 1885 R. xlvi. lx
Jonas, H. M. Brooch, bronze imple-
ments, bust and fibulae from
Royston. 1888 R. xlviii. cxxxviii
Joseph, The Lake of Moeris and the
Patriarch C. vi. 177
Josselin, John, Historiola Collegii
Corporis Christi. Edited by J.
W. Clark. 1880
8vo Pub. No. xvii.
Journeymen Printers' Petition, c. 1611
R. xx. 7
Jugs, Medieval, from Fen Ditton
R. xlii. xxxvi

Jugs (*continued*)
from Littleport R. xli. xiv
Terra-cotta, from Fen Ditton
R. xliv. cxxix
xvi. century stone ware
Pr. vii. 169
Jukes-Browne, A. J., Flint implements
found at Helwan, near Cairo (1
plate). 1877 C. iv. 85
Jupiter Dodonæus, Cameo representing
C. v. 183
Justus, Acts of the Martyr C. i. 191
Jutland, Flint implements from
R. xxxvi. 16

Kaetz, P., Letter to J. Siberch
Pr. vii. 186
Kent. See *Lillecherch. Ospringe*
Kerrich, R. E. Letter of Charles
Rogerson, concerning the christen-
ing of the Duke of York. 1857
R. xviii. 8
Tract relating to the fairs of Bury
St Edmund's and Sturbridge.
1857 R. xviii. 8
MS. verses relative to Oxford and
Cambridge. 1858 R. xix. 7
Impressions from ancient seals.
1859 R. xix. 7
Enamelled plate representing the
Last Judgement. 1859 R. xx. 7
Contemporary portrait of Charles I.
1860. R. xx. 8
MS. of Manner of burienge of Great
Persons in ancient tymes. 1863
R. xxii. 6
City of Magdeburg, and the tomb of
Eadgyth, daughter of Edward the
Elder. 1863 R. xxiii. 8
Copies by Sir Henry Unton of the
correspondence between Q. Eliza-
beth and K. Henry IV. of France,
1596. 1864 R. xxiv. 7
" A poem attempting something up-
on the varieties of the most re-
nowned University of Cambridge,"
1673. 1864. R. xxiv. 8

Kerrich, R. E. (continued)
Letters testimonial of the degree of M.A., 6 July 1653, granted to Robert Rogerson of Caius College. 1865   R. xxv. 8
Copy of an inscription on a vase. 1865.   R. xxvi. 7.
Extracts from the Parish Registers of Stratford, Essex, 1561—1763. 1865   R. xxvi. 7
Three medals. 1866   R. xxvi. 8
Extracts from a newspaper on the Downing family and property. 1867   R. xxxiii. 8
Roman vases found near Cambridge. 1869.   R. xxxiii. 20.
Two pieces of Samian ware. 1869   R. xxxiii. 20
Part of a drinking vessel (xvi. cent.?) found in Jesus College. 1869   R. xxxiii. 20
Curiosities found at Great Gransden. 1870   R. xxxiii. 21
Brass clock. 1871   R. xxxiii. 26
Kertch, Lamps   R. xlvi. lxix
Key from Willingham   R. xxxiii. 8
found in the Cam   R. xxxiii. 16
Keys from St Martin's Priory, Dover   R. ix. 7
Keyser, C. F. Mural paintings and other coloured decorations at Chippenham Church, Cambs. 1886   C. vi. 321
Kiln, Roman, at Great Chesterford   R. xl. xxvii; xxxix. xvii
Kilpeck Church   R. x. 6
Kimmins, C. W., Skulls from Harston. 1887   R. xlvii. cvii
King, Lord Chancellor, Letter from Dr Bentley   C. iii. 175
King, C. W., Catalogue of Coins from Shefford, Beds. 1845   4to. Pub. No. x
Statuette representing Spes Vetus (2 plates, and 7 ill.). 1877   C. iv. 67

King, C. W. (continued)
Mummy's treasure recently discovered in the Delta. (4 ill.) 1879   C. iv. 385
The triumph of Constantine. (2 ill.) 1880   C. iv. 391
Engraved gems of early Christian work. (4 ill.) 1880   C. v. 1
"Stampare a conio." How did the Romans strike their medallions? (3 ill.) 1881   C. v. 33
Two unpublished Christian gem-types. (16 ill.) 1881   C. v. 75
Cameo representing Jupiter Dodonaeus. 1882   C. v. 183
Etruscan mirrors, with engraved reverses. (7 plates and 1 ill.) 1882   C. v. 185
Onyx cameo of Marcia in the character of Omphale. (1 ill.) 1883   C. v. 233
Silver statuette of Fortuna Nemesis. (6 ill.) 1883   C. v. 273
The signet of Eros. (2 ill.) 1884   C. v. 362
Epitaph of M. Verrius Flaccus. 1886   C. vi. 313
Gnostic gems. (1 plate) 1887   C. vi. 347
The fall of Capaneus; An Etruscan Intaglio. 1888   C. vi. 378
King's College. See Cambridge
King's Lynn, On the port of   R. xlviii. cxl
Mantel-piece   R. xlviii. cxl
The making of   Pr. viii. 60
Kirkby Wharfe, Stone R. xliv. cxxxiii
Kirkwall, Orkney Islands, Bronze figure   Pr. vii. 13
Kirtling, chantry at   C. i. 213
Knapwell, Roman coins R. xxxvii. xiii
Knife found in the Cam R. xxxiv. 10
from Jesus College Garden   R. xxiii. 7
from Luzern   R. xxxvi. 21
Knife-handle found in the Thames   R. xxxvi. 21

Knights Templars   R. x. 6
Knives from Barrington   R. xli. xii

Labourer's passes, Seals for
        R. x. 7 : xvii. 10; C. i. 281
Laclianus, Coin   C. v. 225
Lake-dwellings, Model   R. xxxiii. 25
    of Moringen, Stones   R. xxxiii. 36
    of Lake of Neuchatel   R. xxxvi. 9
    Pottery   R. xlii. li
Lakenheath, Millstones   R. xl. xx
    Ring and carving   R. xlv. 7
'lam,' To   R. xxxviii. xiii
Lambeth Palace Library, Salisbury
    Primer or Horae, 1494, in.
                                         C. iii. 237
Lamp, English, dug up in Petty Cury
                                         R. xli. xiii
    from Syracuse   R. xxxvi. 22
    Roman, from Bethlehem
                                         R. xxxvi. 11
    Roman, from Biggleswade
                                         R. xlvii. xcviii
Lamps from Kertch, Terra-cotta
                                         R. xlvi. lxix
Lancashire. See Heysham. Winwick
Landbeach, History of the parish, by
    W. K. Clay. 1861
                                         8vo. Pub. No. vi
    Bell   R. xxxvi. 9
    Terrier of, by Archbishop Parker
                                         R. xlii. lxxx
    Church   C. iv. 245
Land-measures in the Channel Islands
                                         C. vi. 305
    in Domesday   R. xlv. ix
    the Acre   R. xlviii. cxxxiv
    Units of measurement in Domesday
                                         R. xlii. xxxviii
Lane, Dr Thos., Indulgence R. xx. 7
    Will   R. xx. 7
Lang, J. T., on G. F. Browne's paper
    on Altar slab of St Benedict's
    Church. 1889   Pr. vii. 92
Langton, Bp John, Documents from
    the Rolls Office concerning
                                         R. xix. 7

Lany, Edward, Letter to Dr Ashton
                                         C. ii. 195
'lap,' To   R. xxxviii. xiii
Lapland, Runic Calendar   C. iv. 17
Latchmore, F., British coins from
    Hitchin, 1890   Pr. vii. 152
Latham, H., Extracts from the Trinity
    Hall MS "Warren's Book." 1880
                                         R. xi. xxi
Latin Words, List of unusual
                                         R. xxxiii. 15
    Study of Medieval Glossaries
                                         R. xliv. cxxv
Law, J. K.   Curiosities found at
    Christ's College (forged). 1870
                                         R. xxxiii. 25
Lawrence, St, Seal representing, from
    Bottisham Fen   R. xxxiii. 20
Lead-mines of Charterhouse on Mendip,
    Roman signets found
                                         C. iv. 277
Leaden vessels from Willingdon,
    Sussex   R. xxxix. 18
    at Trinity College and Westley
    Waterless   R. xxxix. xiv
Ledsham Church, Carving
                                         R. xlvi. lxviii
Legge, Dr., Tragedy of Richardus
    Tertius, 1579-80   C. i. 347
    Dr Legge's Building, Caius College :
    Musea or Studiola   C. iii. 177
Leicester, Rt. Dudley, Earl of. Sig-
    nature and seal   R. xix. 8
Leicestershire. See Rothley. Whit-
    wick
Lely, Sir Peter, Portrait of Duke of
    Monmouth   R. xvi. 9
Lettou, John, Book printed by
                                         Pr. vii. 190
Leverton, Churchwardens' accounts at
                                         R. xxv. 8
Lewis, S. S., Bronze statuette found
    at Earith. (2 plates and 1 ill.)
    1870   C. iii. 231
    Bronze ram now in the Museum at
    Palermo. (1 ill.) 1871
                                         C. iii. 259

Lewis, S. S. (*continued*)

Exhibits model of the Lake pile-dwellings. 1871 R. xxxiii. 25

Roman Pocillum found near Storey's Almshouses. 1871 R. xxxiii. 27

Denarius of Hadrian. 1871 R. xxxiii. 27

Bronze ornament on vessel from Farndale. 1872 R. xxxiii. 30

Paterae of Samian ware. 1872 R. xxxiii. 31

Back of a large skull. 1872 R. xxxiii. 31

Olla of white ware from Croydon. 1872 R. xxxiii. 31

Narrow-necked bottle, or ampulla, from Croydon. 1872 R. xxxiii. 31

Silver seal. 1872 R. xxxiii. 31

Spur of the xv. century. 1872 R. xxxiii. 31

Macedonian Philippus. 1872 R. xxxiii. 35

Electrotype of a die of a Gaulish coin from Aventicum. 1872 R. xxxiii. 35

British gold coin of the Whaddon Chase find. 1872 R. xxxiii. 35

Merchants' mark on the font in the Church at Barnard Castle. 1872 R. xxxiii. 36

Coin of Constantine the Great. 1872 R. xxxiii. 36

Head of Livia in the character of Ceres, from a gem. 1872 R. xxxiii. 36

Two lacustrine axes. 1873 R. xxxiii. 36

Stones from the pile-dwellings of Moringen. 1873 R. xxxiii. 36

Reproduction of a javelin. 1873 R. xxxiii. 36

Clay object and oak pale, from a pile-dwelling on the lake of Neuchatel. 1873 R. xxxvi. 9

Roman coins found at Barnham. 1873 R. xxxvi. 10

Lewis, S. S. (*continued*)

Engraving of a reindeer, scratched on a reindeer's rib, from Thäingen. 1874 R. xxxvi. 10

Bronze socket-celt found at Willingham. 1874 R. xxxvi. 10

Gallic staters found in France. 1874 R. xxxvi. 10

Roman lamp and vases found at Bethlehem. 1874 R. xxxvi. 11

Bronze medal, etc. 1874 R. xxxvi. 14

Three statuettes found at Tanagra. 1874. 2 plates C. iii. 303

Bronze figure of Mercury. 1874 R. xxxvi. 13

Intaglio gems. 1874 R. xxxvi. 13

Flint implements from Jutland. 1875 R. xxxvi. 16

Brass signet with the head of John the Baptist in a charger. 1875 R. xxxvi. 16.

Green jasper, probably of xiii. century. 1875 R. xxxvi. 20

Lamp from Syracuse. 1876 R. xxxvi. 22

A seated andro-sphinx, from near Canosa. 1876 R. xxxvi. 22

Intaglio bust in Roman glass-paste, probably of Prince Charles Edward. 1876 R. xxxvi. 22

Bronze statuette from Grosseto. 1876 R. xxxvi. 23

A silver fibula. 1876 R. xxxvi. 27

A shekel of the year Five. 1876. (1 ill.) C. iv. 9

Roman coins from Knapwell. 1877 R. xxxvii. xiii

Romano-British pottery from Haslingfield. 1877 R. xxxvii. xii

Bronze coins designed in satire on the Prisoner of Sedan, 1870—1. 1877 R. xxxviii. xi

Four gems exhibited by Canon Scarth. 1877 R. xxxviii. x

Lewis, S. S. (*continued*)
A five franc piece (Mac-Mahon).
1877. (1 ill.) R. xxxviii. xi
Glass vase containing human blood,
from Anstey, Herts. 1878
R. xxxviii. xviii
Fragment of an alabaster figure from
Papworth Everard Church. 1879
R. xl. xii
Skull and three vases found in a
cemetery at Steeple Morden.
1879 R. xl. xii
Roman signets from the lead-mines
of Charterhouse on Mendip.
1879. (15 ill.) C. iv. 277
Inscribed vase, found at Guilden
Morden. 1879. (1 plate and 2
ill.) C. iv. 337
Bronze figure of Mercury. 1880
R. xl. xli
Terra-cotta vessels from Cyprus.
1880 R. xl. xx
Groat of Perkin Warbeck. 1880.
(1 ill.) R. xl. xx
Use of the tally. 1880. (1 plate)
R. xl. xxix
On Lamp exhibited by Mr Redfern.
1880 R. xli. xiii
Offa's lane in Bedford. 1880
R. xli. xiv
Portrait of Homer upon an unpub-
lished coin of Nicaea in Bithynia.
1881. (1 ill.) C. v. 41
Drawing of the statue of Athena
Nikephoros. 1881 R. xli. xix
Pottery rings from Lakes of Bienne
and Neuchatel. 1882 R. xlii. li
Plated denarius of Trajan found
near Cavendish College. 1883
R. xliv. cvii
Pre-historic pottery from South
Utah. 1883 R. xliv. cvii
Denarius of Trajan found near
Cavendish College. 1884
R. xliv. cxxiv
Medal struck at Paris, 1871. 1884
R. xliv. cxxiv

Lewis, S. S. (*continued*)
Copy of the medal commemorating
the silver wedding of the Crown-
Prince Frederick of Prussia. 1884
R. xliv. cxxiv
Fibula from Burwell. 1884
R. xliv. cxxviii
First brass coin of Marcus Aurelius.
1884 R. xlv. vii
Terra-cotta lamps from Kertch.
1886 R. xlvi. xlix
Gallic Gold coins. 1890
Pr. vii. 135
Death, Speeches commemorative
of him, by T. McK. Hughes,
E. C. Clark, C. C. Babington,
R. Bowes, G. W. Fitch, W. M.
Fawcett and J. W. Clark. 1891
Pr. vii. 286
Lewis, Mrs. S. S., Nawamees in the
peninsula of Sinai. 1892
Pr. viii. 61
Samian ware. 1892 Pr. viii. 283
Lewis Collection, Corpus College,
Christian engraved gem
Pr. vii. 171
Four Gnostic gems C. vi. 347
Notes on the Collection
Pr. viii. 57
Lex Wisigothica, A seventh century
leaf of the C. vi. 337
Liber Archidiaconi Eliensis
R. xxv. 8 ; xxxiii. 7
Liber Gratiarum, A R. xxxiii. 13
Libere Tenentes, Virgatae, and Caru-
cae in Domesday, etc.
Pr. vi. 17
Libraries, Ancient, (1) Christ church,
Canterbury, (2) Citeaux, Clair-
vaux, (3) Zutphen, Enkhuizen
Pr. viii. 359
Books printed on vellum, in Colleges
and University of Cambridge, by
S. Sanders. 1878
8vo. Pub., No. xv
Chained, at Cesena, Wells and
Guildford Pr. viii. 1

Libraries (continued)
Chained, at Zutphen   R. xlvi. 69
Church   R. vi. 12
Church and Parochial   C. i. 33
Extracts from Letters on MSS. in
College Libraries, Cambridge
Pr. viii. 6
Medieval, with special reference to
book-cases   R. xlv. xxxviii
Medieval and Collegiate: System
for storing and delivering books
R. xxxvii. ix
Library of the Abbey of St Edmund's
at Bury, by M. R. James. 1895
8vo Pub. No. xxviii
See also Book-cases. Catalogues
Lichfield Cathedral, Discoveries in the
Choir   R. xxi. 6
Seal of Chapter   R. xxvi. 8
Lillecherch, Kent, Mortuary roll of the
House of St Mary's
R. xxxiii. 19
Limber, Wm., of Chesterton, Token
R. xli. xii
Lincoln, A.-S. Fibula mould
R. xli. xix
Sculptured stone   R. xlv. xxx
Lincolnshire. See Caistor. Croyland.
Great Cotes. Leverton. Lincoln.
Newnham. Revesby
Linton Church, Discoveries at
Pr. vii. 15
Lion, Figure of, in Brunswick
R. xxxvi. 16
Marble, from Jerusalem
R. xxv. 8
Litchfield, Mr., Supposed antique
found at Hardwick, etc. 1848
R. viii. 6
British coins. 1848   R. viii. 6
"Littera Fraternitatis concessa...
Juarii filio de Insula de Ysland,"
preserved at Canterbury
.   C. iv. 401
Littleport, Court Rolls of the Manor
C. iv. 97
Remains from   R. xli. xiv

Liverpool Merchants, Ring Money of,
used on West Coast of Africa
R. xli. xxv
Livett, J. J. W., The Cistercian
monastery at Whitwick. 1888
R. xlviii. cxxxvii
Livia as Ceres, from a gem
R. xxxiii. 36
Lleithvaen, Grass in Churchyard, a
cure for Hydrophobia
R. xxxviii. xii
Loch Maree, Stakes and pottery from
Wattle-hut   Pr. vii. 185
Londesborough Park, Yorkshire,
Beads, etc.   R. xliv. cxxix
London. Draft of a conveyance in
1780 of the house in Cornhill in
which Thomas Gray was born
R. xxiii. 7
Maces of the Ward of Bread Street
R. xxxix. xiv
Sculptured stones in Guildhall, Brit-
ish Museum, etc. R. xliv. cxxxii
See British Museum. Lambeth
Lopez's History: Account of Trini-
tarian House in Cambridge
R. xxi. 8
Lord's Day, Attempts to pass an Act
for the better observance of
R. xxiii. 9
Lorrain, Hanzelet, La Pyrotechnie de
R. xxxiii. 36
Lothian, Sculptured stones
R. xliv. cx
Lough Glyn, Stone implement
R. xxxiii. 13
Luard. H. R. Diary of Edward Rudd,
1709—1720; with several unpub-
lished letters of Richard Bentley.
1860   8vo Pub. No. v
Correspondence of Richard Porson.
1867   8vo Pub. No. viii
Impression of a seal purporting to
be that of Galatius Episcopus Sar-
sinatensis. 1856   R. xvii. 9
Rare edition of Tzetzes, circa 1490—
1522. 1858   R. xviii. 8

Luard, **H. R.** (*continued*)
Volume relating to the trial of John
Hampden. 1858   R. xviii. 8
Extracts from the annals of Tewkes-
bury relative to the Stadinger.
1863   R. xxiii. 8
Visitation of the Churches of Pelham
Furneaux **and Brent** Pelham,
Herts., 1297. **1865**   C. iii. 53
Charter of **A.D.** 1137 in confirmation
of the privileges of the Monastery
of Eye, Suffolk. 1866 R. xxvi. 8
Fragment of Ammonites biplex,
bearing a curious resemblance to
a mole. 1867   R. xxxiii. 10
Letter **from** Bishop Bale to Arch-
bishop Parker. 1867
     C. iii. 157
Letter from Dr Bentley to Lord
Chancellor King. 1867
     C. iii. 175
Copper two-penny piece, 1797. 1867
     R. xxxiii. 11
List of unusual Latin words. 1869
     R. xxxiii. 15
Indenture for erection of rood-loft
in Great St Mary's. 1869
     R. xxxiii. 16
Earthenware-pot found in St Mary's
passage. 1869   R. xxxiii. 16
Keys found in the Cam. 1869
     R. xxxiii. **16**
A Chancellor's Gold Medal **gained**
in 1810. 1870   R. xxxiii. **20**
Letter to the University from Thomas
Beaufort, Duke of Exeter. 1872
     C. iii. 273
Coins of the Empress Crispina,
found in Cambridge. 1872.
     R. xxxiii. 33
Coins, Indian, dated 1833. **1872**
     R. xxxiii. **35**
Coins, **Hamburg and Roman.** 1873
     R. **xxxiii. 37**
List of Documents in the University
Registry, from 1266—1544. **1876**
     C. iii. **385**

Luard, H. R. (*continued*)
Remarks on Dr Bruce's History of
Hadrian's Wall. 1882
     R. xlii. xlvi
Cross at Sawston. 1882
     R. xliii. lxxvi
On H. Middleton's Paper on the
Legend of Atlantis. 1883
     R. xliii. lxxxix
On H. F. Wilson's Objects of inte-
rest from Trinity Coll. 1885
     R. xlv. xxxi
On W. G. Searle's paper on Ingulf's
Croyland. 1891   Pr. vii. 210
Death, reference by the President.
1891   Pr. vii. 286
Lumby, J. R., List of Vestments, etc.,
from the Churchwardens' book **of**
Bassingbourne. 1868
     R. xxxiii. 11, 13
Deed **of** xvii. century relating to
some inhabitants of Girton. 1870
     R. xxxiii. 21
Pair of hobblers from the Barnwell
gravel hole. 1871. R. xxxiii. 27
Lunn, J. R. Memoir of Caleb Parn-
ham, B.D., **sometime** Fellow and
Tutor of St John's College. 2nd
Edn., enlarged. 1883
     8vo Pub. **No.** xxi
Luzern, Knife   R. xxxvi. 20
Lyng Church, Norfolk, **Altar Cloth**
     Pr. vii. 4
Lynn. *See King's Lynn*
Lysons' Cambridgeshire: Statement
concerning Malketon   R. xii. 7

M., G., a wandering Flemish artist of
xv—xvi. century, Engravings of
     C. iii. 247
Macalister, Alex., Human Bones from
Burwell. 1884
     R. xliv. cxxviii
Visceral or so-called Canopic jar.
1884   R. xliv. cxxxi
Inscribed block of clay from Thebes.
1885   R. xlv. xxxix

Macalister, Alex. (*continued*)
Inscription containing the name of
  Amasis. 1885   R. XLVI. lxiii
Fragment of a statue bearing the
  name of Psammis. 1885
               R. XLVI. lxiv
Egyptian skulls. 1886
               R. XLVII. cx
Presidential Address, 1887.
  R. XLVIII. cxxxiii : 1889 C. VII. 72
Six Egyptian skulls. 1887
               R. XLVIII. cxxxvi
Roman coins, and bronze, iron, and
  bone articles from Hauxton.
  1888   R. XLVIII. cxxxvi
Roman pottery found on the
  Madingley Road. 1888
               Pr. VII. 1
Egyptian Stele. 1888   Pr. VII. 3
Collection of Egyptian Skulls of the
  xxvi. dynasty. 1889
               Pr. VII. 17
Two unpublished Egyptian stelae.
  1892   Pr. VIII. 317
Macalister, Alex. and T. McK. Hughes.
  See *Hughes*
Macalister, R. A. S. Killeen Cormaic,
  Kildare. 1894   Pr. VIII. 337
Macedonian coins. See *Coins*
Maces in the University Registry
               R. XXXIX. xiv
  of the Esquire Bedells, and Yeoman
    Bedell   C. IV. 207
  of the Town of Cambridge
               R. XXXIX. xiv
  of the Ward of Bread Street, London
               R. XXXIX. xiv
Madelaine, La, Stone implements
  from   R. XXXVIII. xix
Magdeburg, City of, and the Tomb of
  Eadgyth   R. XXIII. 8
Magic, Fragments of a Graeco-Egyp-
  tian work on   8vo Pub. No. II
Magnentius, Coin   R. XL. xvii
Magnússen, E., On an Early Runic
  Calendar found in Lapland, 1866.
  (1 plate and 6 ill.) 1877   C. IV. 17

Magnússen, E. (*continued*)
Description of a Norwegian Calen-
  dar. (1 plate and 6 ill.) 1878
               C. IV. 129
"Littera Fraternitatis concessa Wyt-
  frido Juarii filio de Insula de
  Ysland," preserved at Canterbury.
  1880   C. IV. 401
Runic Calendars. (18 plates) 1888
  C. VI. 368 : Remarks by W. W.
  Skeat   R. XLVIII. 136
On the Stone of Jaellinge. (1 plate
  and 1 ill.) 1889   Pr. VII. 18
Maiden Way, Cumberland, as a Roman
  Road   C. VI. 41
Mainz Cathedral, Photographs
               R. XXXVIII. xiv
Malketon, Statement in Lysons' Cam-
  bridgeshire concerning   R. XII. 7
Malton. See *Malketon*
Malvern, Great, Gold coin
               Pr. VII. 135
Manea, Antiquities   Pr. VIII. 87
Manea Fen, Skeleton of a stag
               Pr. VII. 2
Manning, C. R., Seal of John Salle.
  1887   C. VI. 345
Mantel-piece from Lynn, oaken
               R. xlviii. cxl
Mantua, Sculptured stones
               R. XLVII. cxii
Mantuan Vase, Earliest Account of
               R. XLIII. lxxvii
  at Brunswick   C. III. 307
Manumissions of Serfs from Records
  of King's College   C. I. 359
Manuscripts, Waldensian, recovered
               C. II. 203
  in College Libraries   R. VIII. 6
March, Photograph of Stone Imple-
  ment from New Park   R. XLV. vii
Marcia in the character of Omphale,
  Onyx cameo   C. V. 233
Maree, Loch, Stakes and pottery
               Pr. VII. 185
Margaret, the Lady. See *Beaufort*
Marius, Coin of   C. V. 225

Mark's, St, Gospel, Uncial MS of
R. **xxii.** 6

Markaunt, Thos., Catalogue **of Books**
given to Corpus College
4to Pub. No. iii.

Marr, J. E., British vase and human
bones found at Fen Ditton. 1877
R. xxxvii. xii

and T. M�‘K. Hughes. See *Hughes*

Marshall, W., Roman coin from Ely.
1853 R. xiv. 6

Court Rolls of the Manor of Littleport, in the Isle of Ely. 1878
C. iv. 97 ; R. xxxviii. xvi

Account of the Old Chapel, Sidney
College, by Jas. Essex, 1776.
1878 R. xxxviii. xvi

Canoe found in the Fen-Peat, **near**
Magdalen Bend, on the Ouse,
Norfolk. 1878. (4 ill.) **C. iv.** 195

Martin, C. T., Deeds, 1439 to 1646,
found at Wilbraham Parva. 1888
R. xlviii. cxxxviii

Martin, Dr Edward, Letter to William
Bray C. ii. 149

Martin's, St, **Priory,** Dover, Pillar in
Church R. ix. 7

Matrix, **Bone,** from St John's College.
R. xiii. 6

Maudslay, A. P., **Explorations in Central** America. **1883**
R. xliv. cxviii

Maximianus Hercules, Coins of. See
Coins : Roman

Mayor, J. E. B., Unpublished Letters
of M. Prior and R. Ascham. 1854
R. xiv. 7 ; C. i. 99

MS. autobiography of **Matthew**
Robinson. 1855 R. xv. **9**

The personal history **of** Cranmer.
1855 R. xv. 9

Extracts from Baker's MSS relating
to the election of Vice-Chancellor.
1855 R. xv. 10

Desirability of the publication **of**
MSS. relating to Cambridge. **1855**
R. xv. 10

Mayor, J. E. B. (*continued*)

Letter relating to the life of Cudworth, addressed to the University by J. T. Mosheim ; together
with the answer of the University.
Extracted from the Baker MSS.
1856 C. i. 195

Dr Richard Sibbes. **1856** C. i. 253

Extracts from an unpublished autobiography of Roger North. 1857
R. xviii. 7

Letters from Robert Booth of **St**
John's College, to Dr Claiton,
Master, concerning the Second
Court. 1858 C. i. 343

Thomas Morton, Bishop of Durham.
1859 C. iii. 1

Letters of Archbishop Williams and
others, with the building accounts
of St John's College Library.
1859 C. ii. 25 ; iii. 61 ; R. xx. 7

Receipts for the payments of **Peter's**
pence, 1523 and 1529. 1860
R. xx. 8

Letter from Dr Goodman **to Dr
Gwynne** concerning **copyright,
1616.** 1860 R. **xx.** 7

Letters from George Acworth **to**
Archbishops Pole and Parker.
1861 C. ii. 79

Letter from Bishop Bedell to Sir
Nath. Rich. 1861 C. ii. 95

Letters from Robert Bouth and
John Bois, preserved in St John's
College Treasury. 1859
C. ii. 139

Letter of Godfrey Goodman, with
materials for his life C. ii. 113

Extracts from Uffenbach's Travels,
describing his visit to Cambridge,
in 1710. **1861** R. xxii. 6

Orations of R. **Croke.** 1862
R. **xxii.** 7

F. Burmanni Itineris **Anglicana**
Acta Diurna. An account of his
visit to England, 1702. 1862
R. **xxii.** 8

Mayor, J. E. B. (*continued*)
Inventory of Books, plate and other goods belonging to St John's College, 1520–44. 1862 R. xxiii. 7
Contents of Bp. Fisher's box of papers at St John's College. 1864 R. xxiv. 8
MS. form of prayer at the consecration of Peterhouse chapel by Archbishop Sancroft. 1864 R. xxiv. 9 .
The "Archdeacon's Book" in Caius College. 1864 R. xxv. 8
Extracts from Burmanni Itineris Anglicana Acta Diurna (Burmann's visit to Cambridge, 1702, with particulars of the Hall and Chapel in Trinity). 1865 R. xxv. 8
A small marble Lion from Jerusalem. 1865 R. xxv. 8
Dutch records preserved at the Hague. 1865 R. xxv. 9
A Letter-Book of St John's College. 1865 R. xxv. 9
Bonds not to procure dispensations from Rome. 1868 R. xxxiii. 15
The first set of Statutes of St John's College. 1868 R. xxxiii. 15
Old register containing Bp. Fisher's funeral sermon on the Lady Margaret. 1868 R. xxxiii. 15
Plans and other documents connected with the second court of St John's College. 1868 R. xxxiii. 15
Documents from St John's College. 1869 R. xxxiii. 18, 19
Quatuor orationes autore Pawlet St John. 1870 R. xxxiii. 36
Coins of Edward VI., Elizabeth and Charles I. 1872 R. xxxiii. 36
Moise du Soul (Moses Solanus) M.A., by Royal Mandate, 1701. 1882 C. v. 167
Mead, G. B., Visits of James I. to Newmarket. 1863 C. ii. 295

Medals, Bronze, 1794 Pr. vii. 252
Bronze, of time of Justinian Rhinotmetus, vii. century R. xxxvi. 14
Bronze, commemorating Silver Wedding of Frederick William, Crown Prince of Germany R. xliv. cxxiv
Chancellor's Gold, 1810 R. xxxiii. 20
Chinese University R. xxxvi. 11
commemorating Lord Royston attaining his majority R. xxxiii. 25
Gold, from Stowmarket R. xxxiii. 13
Installation of Prince Albert R. xxxiii. 27
of Queen Anne, 1704 Pr. vii. 9
of John Frederic, Elector of Saxony R. xxvi. 8
on the marriage of Vladislaus IV., King of Poland R. xxvi. 8
on the accession of Christina, Q. of Sweden R. xxvi. 8
Parisian, 1871, found in the ruins of the Tuileries R. xliv. cxxiv
Silver, by D. Hood of Cambridge, 1796 R. xxxiii. 11
Medallion, French R. xxxvi. 21
from Burwell R. ix. 7
from York R. xxxvi. 25
Medallions, How did the Romans strike their? C. v. 33
Medals of the Stuarts R. xlii. xxxvii
of Cambridge, by W. G. Searle. 1871 8vo Pub. No. xii.
See also *Tokens*
Medrásen, The, in Algeria C. iii. 379
Megalithic remains in S. Brittany R. xxvi. 8
Meldreth, Chantry at C. i. 213
Mendip, Roman Signets found in leadmines of Charterhouse C. iv. 277
Mentone, Archaeological notes on the neighbourhood R. xliii. lxxix
Mepal, Purchase of the Manor and Advowson Pr. vii. 131

Mepal Fen, Two British funereal vases
R. xx. 7
Merchants' mark, Medieval
C. iv. 187
on font at Barnard Castle Church
R. xxxiii. 36
Mercury, Bronze figure, from Fen-
stanton R. xl. xvi
Bronze figure R. xxxvi. 13 ; xl. xli
Mertola, Christian inscription, c. A.D.
546 R. xlvii. cviii ; Pr. vii. 7
Mexican Coins R. xxxiii. 36
Mexico. See Arizona.
Middleton, Henry, Legend of Atlantis.
1883 R. xliii. lxxxvii
Middleton, J. H., The silks in which
St Cuthbert's body was wrapped.
1886 R. xlvii. xcv
Five bronze figures in the Museum.
1886 R. xlvii. c
On M. Rule's paper on Deerhurst
Church. 1886 R. xlvii. ciii
A reliquary found in a Church in
Yorkshire. 1887 R. xlvii. cviii
Two Christian Inscriptions from
Mertola and Alemquer. 1887
R. xlvii. cviii
The temple of Apollo. 1888
R. xlviii. cxxxvii
On G. F. Browne's paper on Pam-
pisford Church. 1888
R. xlviii. cxxxix
Altar-cloth from Lyng Church, Nor-
folk. (2 ill.) 1888 Pr. vii. 4
Chasubles from Sawston Hall. 1889
Pr. vii. 10
Choir-stalls from Brampton Church,
Hunts. 1889. (1 plate and 1 ill.
in text.) Pr. vii. 28
A blue-glazed Oenochoe of Ptole-
maic manufacture. 1889. 1 plate.
Pr. vii. 72
on G. F. Browne's Sculptured stones.
1889. Pr. vii. 92
The House of the Veysy family.
1889 Pr. vii. 93
Fragments of alabaster retables

Middleton, J. H. (continued)
from Milton and Whittlesford.
1889. (4 plates) Pr. vii. 106
Stone-ware jug of xvi. century.
1890 Pr. vii. 169
Christian engraved gem in the Lewis
Collection. 1890. 1 Illustration
in text Pr. vii. 171
Signet ring of the xv. Century.
1890 Pr. vii. 193
On the Lewis Collection at Corpus
Christi College. 1892 Pr. viii. 57
Mildenhall, Bronze implement
R. xi. 7
Grain-rubber R. xxi. 8
Pottery and Roman coin from West
Row Fen R. xliii. lxxi
Worked flints R. xxxix. xi
Mile, The English Statute, and the
smaller measures of length
C. iv. 267
Milestones on the road from Cam-
bridge to London C. iv. 268
Miller, S. H., Alleged idolatry in the
Fens. 1886 R. xlvii. ciii
Millington, W., First Provost of King's
College C. i. 287
Millington, Arms C. i. 239
Mill-stones from Caldecote and Caxton
R. xliv. cxxvii
from Lakenheath R. xl. xx
Roman, from Great Eversden
R. xliii. lxxxiii
Milton, John, Seal R. xii. 8
Milton, History of the parish, by
W. K. Clay. 1869
8vo Pub. No. xi.
Alabaster retable Pr. vii. 106
Mirror, Origin of the word
R. xliii. lxxi
Mirrors, Etruscan, with engraved re-
verses C. v. 185
Moats and Moated Halls at Coton, &c.
C. iii. 287
at Caxton R. xliii. lxxxiii
Mœris, Lake of, and the Patriarch
Joseph C. vi. 177

Moise du Soul (Moses Solanus)
C. v. 167
Mold. Offa's dyke from Parish of Mold
to the sea R. xviii. 9
Monastic buildings, Arrangement
R. vii. 3
Money, Copper, used in trade, west
coast of Africa R. xli. xxv
Monmouth, James, Duke of, Engraving, by A. Blooteling R. xvi. 9
Montpensier, Ring C. iv. 181
Monuments from Central America
R. xliii. lxxxviii
More, John, Marriage and children
C. iii. 199
Moringen, Stone from pile-dwellings
R. xxxiii. 36
Mortarium from Ely R. xli. xxv
Mortlock, J. G., An oaken mantel-piece
from Lynn. 1888 R. xlviii. cxl
Morton, Thos., Bishop of Durham,
Materials for life C. iii. 1
Mortars, Three R. xlviii. cxxxiii
Metal, from site of Post Office
R. xlv. xiii
Mortuary Roll sent forth by the Prior
and Convent of Ely C. i. 125
of the House of St Mary's Lillecherch R. xxxiii. 19
Mosheim, J. J., Letter to the University C. i. 195
Moule, C. W., On death of Rev. S. S.
Lewis. 1891 Pr. vii. 288
Mounds resembling Tumuli, Formation
of natural R. xxxvi. 26
Mount Sorrel, Ancient well
Pr. viii. 133
Mullinger, J. B., On R. Bowes' paper
on University Printers. 1884
R. xliv. cxxiii
On the Rev. E. G. de S. Wood's
paper on Stamford University.
1888 Pr. vii. 2
Mummy's treasures recently discovered
in the Delta C. iv. 385
Mural Paintings at Chippenham
Church C. vi. 321

Musea or Studiola in Caius College
C. iii. 177
Music in Ashwell Church R. xxii. 7
' Mutton-Hole,' Origin of the name
R. xlii. xlix

Napoleon III., Coin satirizing, 1870–
71 R. xxxviii. xi
Nawâmees in the Peninsula of Sinai
Pr. viii. 61
Nayland, Cinerary Urn R. xlvii. 105
Naylor, T. H., Impression of an ecclesiastical seal. 1875
R. xxxvi. 21
Fifteen tokens found at Chesterton.
1876 R. xxxvi. 22
Fresco in Chesterton Church. (1
plate.) 1876 C. iv. 3
Frescoes in Chesterton Church. 1877
R. xxxviii. xi
Antiquities, mostly found at Chesterton. 1879 R. xxxviii. xvi
The mace-heads of the town of Cambridge. 1879 R. xxxix. xiv
Piece of a medieval brass book-clasp
from Chesterton. 1880
R. xli. xiii
Chalice formerly belonging to Rockland Church, probably xvi. century. 1881 R. xli. xviii
Chalice belonging to the Church of
St Andrew the Great, Cambridge.
1881 R. xli. xviii
Case of engravings, two bronze
medals, a reprint of Eikon Basilike, and other memorials of the
Stuarts. 1881 R. xlii. xxxvii
Necklace, Amber, from Wilbraham
R. viii. 6
Nero, Coin of R. xxxvii. ix
Nero, Drusus, Coin R. xlv. xxxi
Nerva, Coin R. xlviii. cxxxvi
Neuchatel, Objects from pile dwellings
on lake R. xxxvi. 9
Pottery Rings from lake R. xlii. li
Newcastle, Earl of, Letter to, 1641
R. xi. 8

New England, Establishment of printing R. xxvi. 7

Stone implements R. xxxviii. xii

Newman, Thos., Deed from Thos. Hobson R. xxii. 8

Newman, Samuel, Concordance, Baker's copy R. xvii. 10

Newmarch, C. H., Notes on Roman buildings at Cirencester. 1853 C. i. 55

Newmarket, Excavations in neighbourhood R. xlv. xxi

Antiquities Pr. vii. 307

Arrow-head R. xlii. xlii

Axes and other objects R. xxxvi. 21

Bottle R. xliii. lxxvii

Roman coins, &c. R. xliv. cxxi

Visits of K. James I. C. ii. 295

Newnham, Bell found at R. xl. xvi

Newnham, Northants, Fibulae R. xiv. 7

Newport, Essex, Manufactory of Flint Implements R. xxxix. xvi

Newspapers, The first and other early Cambridge Pr. viii. 349

New Testament, Gloucester Ridley's account of a Syriac MS C. ii. 219

Latin MS, in Pembroke College Library Pr. viii. 221

Uncial MS of St Mark's Gospel R. xxii. 6

Newton, Sir Isaac, Two Letters to the Mayor of Chester, 1698-9 C. iii. 153

His schoolmaster, Henry Stokes C. ii. 161

Newton, Samuel (Alderman of Cambridge), Diary, 1662-1717, edited by J. E. Foster. 1890 8vo Pub. No. xxiii

Diary R. xlvi. lxx

Newton, Roman Antiquities Pr. vii. 185

Nicaea, Coin of R. xx. 7 : C. v. 41

Nineveh, Cuneiform Inscription R. xliii. lxxxiii

Nonae Rolls, as they relate to Cambridge C. i. 7

Norfolk, Survey of Manors Pr. vi. 17

See Buckenham. Castle Acre. Cromer. Diss. Elmham. Fens. Haddiscoe. Hunstanton. King's Lynn. Lyng. Ouse. Rockland. Swaffham. Thetford. Toft Monks. Wretham

Norfolk squire's Note-book of xvi. and xvii. centuries C. v. 201

Norris, John, founder of the Norrisian Professorship C. ii. 147

North, Roger, Extracts from his unpublished Autobiography R. xviii. 7

Northampton, Triangular bricks R. xlvi. lxix

Northamptonshire. See Arbury. Cold Ashby. Hunsbury. Newnham. Peterborough. Seaton. Sulby Abbey

Northumberland : Whitley

Norwegian Calendar C. iv. 129

Notaries Public, in King's College C. iii. 47

Nottinghamshire. See Stapleford

Nuremberg, Caskets R. viii. 6

Churches R. xii. 7

Oak, Black, from Burwell Fen R. xxxiii. 36

Oakington, Coin of Harthacnut found R. xxiii. 7

Oenochoe of Ptolemaic manufacture Pr. vii. 72

Offa's bridge near Foxton R. xli. xiv

brook, near Foxton R. xli. xiv

Dyke R. xviii. 9 ; xli. xii, xiv

Lane at Bedford R. xli. xiv

Offord, Agreement between Convent of Clugny and farmers of, 1237 R. xlvii. cx

Ogam inscription on Sculptured stone Pr. vii. 88

Oglesby, Jos., Intaglio medallion of Jupiter Ammon, from York. 1876 R. xxxvi. 25

Olla of white ware from Croydon
R. xxxiii. 31
Omphale, Onyx cameo of Marcia as
C. v. 233
Onyx known as the Mantuan Vase, at
Brunswick C. iii. 307
See *Cameo*
Ordesan (Pyrenees) Pottery
R. xxxvii. xii ; xl. xxvi
Orkney Islands. See *Kirkwall*
Ormeshead, Great, Shells and bones
R. xxxiii. 8
Ornament, Bronze, from Farndale
R. xxxiii. 30
Orvieto Cathedral, Flaxman's draw-
ings of Sculptures on the facade
R. xxxvii. x
Orwell, Parish of, and Malton, Cambs.
R. xii. 7
Ospringe, Hospital at, Cartulary
R. xxxiii. 18
Ouse, River, Norfolk, Canoe found near
Magdalen Bend C. iv. 195
Ouse Marches, Canoe R. xxxix. xiii
Over, Chantry C. i. 214
Owen, John, *Printer*, 1701-7
C. vi. 362
Ox, Two varieties of R. xlv. xi
Oxfordshire, "The Three Pigeons"
near Thame, probably the scene
of "She Stoops to Conquer"
R. xliii. lxxi
Oxford and Cambridge, MS verses on
R. xix. 7

Pacific Islands, Weapons, &c.
R. xlviii. cxxxiv
Paddison, Henry, Looped wedge of
bronze from Arkesden. 1875
R. xxxvi. 15
Padua University, Monuments to Cam-
bridge Men Pr. viii. 337
Painting in Cottenham Church
R. xiv. 8
of St Thomas of Canterbury, in
Hauxton Church Pr. viii. 75

Paintings in Teversham Church
R. xliii. lxxii
See also *Frescoes*
Pakefield, Roman coin from
R. xxxvii. ix
Pale, Oaken, from pile dwellings on
Lake of Neuchatel R. xxxvi. 9
Palermo, Bronze Ram in the Museum
C. iii. 259
Palestine. See *Bethlehem*
Paley, F. A., Stone implements from
Lough Glyn. 1868
R. xxxiii. 13
Medal from Stowmarket. 1868
R. xxxiii. 13
Cylindrical stone from Barnwell.
1868 R. xxxiii. 13
Rubbing of inscription on a bell,
1294. 1868 R. xxxiii. 15
Flint weapons found at Grimes
Graves, near Thetford, Norfolk.
1869 R. xxxiii. 16
Coins and tokens, one representing
the "Three Tuns" Inn, Castle
Hill. 1871 R. xxxiii. 26
The west towers of York Minster.
1871 C. iii. 269
Inscription in the Lady Chapel at
Peterborough. 1872 R. xxxiii. 31
Pedigree of the Apthorp family. 1872
R. xxxiii. 36
Old Black Oak from Burwell Fen.
1872 R. xxxiii. 36
Red-deer horn from Burwell Fen.
1872 R. xxxiii. 36
Moats and Moated Halls at Coton,
Grantchester, Barnwell Abbey,
and Fen Ditton ; with remarks
on Manor House and College
boundary walls, fish-ponds, and
Columbaria. 1873 C. iii. 287
Palmer, E. H., The Crook in the right
hand of the figure of Rameses III.
on the cover of his Sarcophagus
in the Fitzwilliam Museum. 1875
C. iii. 383
Palstaves from near Ely R. xxxvi. 9

Pampisford **Church**, Tympanum of
   door   C. VI. 384
   Rectory   C. VI. 384
Papal Legates' process in the case of
   the divorce between Henry VIII.
   and Catharine   R. XXIV. 7
Papworth Everard Church, Figure
                 R. XL. xii
Paris, Medal struck at   R. XLIV. cxxiv
Parish accounts of Boxworth, Suffolk,
   1529-1596   C. I. 265
   Registers of Abington Pigotts
               R. XLVII. cxi
   Registers of Stratford, Essex
               R. XXVI. 7
Parker, Archbishop, Rites **and cere-**
   monies at consecration of
            4to Pub. No. III
   Letter from G. Acworth   C. II. 79
   Letter from Bishop Bale
               C. III. 157
   Terrier of Landbeach   R. XLII. lxxx
Parnham, Caleb, B.D., sometime fellow
   and tutor of **St** John's College.
   Cambridge, Memoir by J. R. Lunn.
   2nd Edn., enlarged, 1883
           8vo Pub. **No. XXI**
Paston, Erasmus, **Brass**   R. **XII.** 8
Paten from Westley **Waterless**
               R. **IX.** 21
Patera in Samian ware, from Ely
               R. XLI. xxv
Paterae of Samian ware   R. XXXIII. 31
Pavement in Exchequer Chamber,
   Exeter   R. VII. **4**
   of encaustic tiles   R. IX. 6
Pearson, John B., Onyx known as the
   Mantuan Vase, in the Grand-
   Ducal Museum, Brunswick. 1875
               C. III. 307
   Bronze figure of a lion in Brunswick.
   1875   R. XXXVI 16
   Relics of the Arctic explorer, Barentz,
   at the Hague. 1877
              R. XXXVII. xi
   Roman monument at Turbia, Mo-
   naco. 1878   R. XXXVIII. xiv

Pearson, John B. (*continued*)
   The Mace of the Ward **of Bread**
   Street, London. 1879
               R. XXXIX. xiv
   Table of distances between different
   towns given by Holinshed in his
   description of England. 1879
               C. IV. 261
   Note 1. On the present English
   statute mile and on the smaller
   measures of length   C. IV. 267
   Note 2. On the mile-stones on
   the road from Cambridge to
   London   C. IV. 268
   Earthen rampart **at** Perekop, at
   the entrance to the Crimea. 1881
               C. V. 47
   Rubbing of brass, giving the date
   29 Feb. 1629, from Preston, Suf-
   folk. 1881   R. XLI. xxii
   Roman wall in S. Germany. 1882
              R. XLII. xlvi
   The "Three Pigeons," near Thame,
   Oxon., probably the scene of "She
   Stoops to Conquer." 1882
              R. **XLIII. lxxi**
   Land measures **known as an acre.**
   1887   R. **XLVIII. cxxxiv**
   Ancient **chapel near How House.**
   1892   Pr. **VIII. 55**
   Assessments of Cambridgeshire,
   1291-1889. 1893   Pr. VIII. 55
Pebble, Perforated, from Ditton
               R. XL. xxvii
Pelham **Furneaux, Visitation of** the
   Church   C. III. 53
Pell, O. C., Libere Tenentes, Virgatae,
   and Carucae in Domesday, and
   in certain ancient MSS., containing surveys of sixty manors in
   the counties of Hereford, Essex,
   Norfolk, Suffolk, Huntingdon, and
   Cambridge; and upon Wara, what
   it probably meant or implied, and
   the prevalent use of the word both
   here and on the continent in
   ancient times. 1884   C. VI. **17**

Pell, O. C. (*continued*)
Land measurements in Domesday.
1884 R. xlv. ix
Gold ring-money from Wilburton
Fen. 1895 R. xlv. xvii
Stag's-horn and the base of its fellow
from Stretham. 1895
R. xlv. xvii
Horn, probably of a bos primi-
genius, from Wilburton, 1895
R. xlv. xvii
Silver spoon (c. 1570 or 1620) from
Wilburton. 1895 R. xlv. xvii
The Domesday geldable Hide, what
it probably was and what it cer-
tainly was not : with an explana-
tion of the Domesday terms Terra
ad Carucam, Carucata, and Virgata,
from information contained in
certain MSS of the xiii. century,
including the Hundred Rolls.
1885 C. vi. 65 ; R. xlv. xviii
Pembroke College. See *Cambridge*
Pendants, Filagree ball R. xli. xxv
Pennsylvania, Barbed Arrow-heads
R. xl. xx
Pentateuch, Age of a Syriac MS
C. ii. 219
Percival, S. G., Presented Romano-
British vase found on Coldham
Common. 1897 R. xxxviii. xi
Presented Glass bottle, with legend
"Tho : Ewin, Cambridge, 1736."
1884 R. xlv. vii
Percy, Alan, Second Master of St
John's, Portrait Pr. viii. 229
Perekop, Earthen rampart C. v. 47
Perkin Warbeck, Groat R. xl. xx
Perthshire. See *Ardoch*
Peru, Two urns R. xl. xxvii
Pre-historic Peruvian stone imple-
ments C. iv. 13
Perugia, Etruscan inscription
Pr. viii. 253
Peshawur Valley, Graeco-Buddhistic
fragments Pr. viii. 148
Peterborough, Coins &c. Pr. vii. 189

Peterborough Cathedral, Inscription
in Lady Chapel. R. xxxiii. 31
Peterhouse. See *Cambridge*
Peter's Pence, Receipts for, 1523 and
1529 R. xx. 8
Petty Cury, Origin of the name
C. i. 63
Pewter plates from Abington Pigotts
R. xlvii. cxi
Pfahlbauten at Concise, Lake of Neu-
chatel R. xxv. 7
Phillips, H. (of Philadelphia), Pre-
sented nine barbed arrow-heads
found in Pennsylvania. 1880
R. xl. xx
Phoenician Glass Bottle R. xxxvi. 15
Pickering Church, Frescoes of St
George and the Dragon
Pr. vii. 131
Pierotti, E., Archaeological studies in
Greece. 1862 R. xxii. 7
Pig, Late medieval, from foundations
of new Post-Office R. xlv. xiii
Pigott, W. G. F., Sepulchral urns from
Wicken. 1880 R. xli. xv
Site of a Roman veteran's holding
at Abington Pigotts, Cambs. (2
ill.) 1886 C. vi. 309
Pewter plates from Abington Pigotts.
1887 R. xlvii. cxi
Fragment of a bowl of Samian
ware. 1887 R. xlvii. cxii
Gold coin of Cunobelin from Abing-
ton Pigotts. 1885 R. xlv. xxxi
Denarius of Nero Drusus from
Abington Pigotts. 1885
R. xlv. xxxi
Coins of Constans and Gratian, and
other objects from Abington
Pigotts. 1885 R. xlv. xxxi
Exhibited a bronze Ring-dial found
at Abington Pigotts. 1890
Pr. vii. 130
On the parish registers of Abington
Pigotts. 1890 Pr. vii. 175
Pile-dwellings. See *Lake-dwellings*
Pilgrim's badge, Imitations R. xxiv. 7

Pilgrims' bottles from site of Post Office
R. xlv. xiii
leaden Ampulla R. xxxiii. 16
Pilton Priory, Devon, Seal R. ix. 8
Pin, Roman, dug up in Petty Cury
R. xli. xiii
Pincushion R. xxxvi. 15
Pistol, xvii. century wheel-lock
R. xxxix. xix
Pius VII., Ornament bearing arms
R. xlviii. cxxxviii
Plantin, La maison, at Antwerp
C. iv. 271
Plaque, Ivory, from Elmham
R. xlvii. c
Plate, sent to Charles I. by Queens'
College C. i. 241
belonging to Margaret Beaufort,
Duchess of Richmond and Derby
R. xxxiii. 19
Specimens of College, by J. J. Smith.
(13 plates.) 1845 4to Pub. No. xi
Plate Exhibition, Catalogue of the
loan collection of Plate exhibited
at the Fitzwilliam Museum, May
8, 9, and 10, 1895, by J. E. Foster
and T. D. Atkinson. 8vo.
Ditto. Illustrated Edition. 16 plates,
and woodcuts. 1896. 252 copies
printed on ordinary paper, 35 on
Japanese paper. 4to.
Plates, Pewter, from Abington Pigotts
R. xlvii. cxi
Pocillum, Roman, found near Storey's
Almshouses R. xxxiii. 27
Poem, Satirical, circa 1320 R. ix. 6
Pole, Archbishop, Letters from G. Ac-
worth C. ii. 79
Popish Recusants, Proclamation concerning R. xxvi. 7
Porson, Richard, formerly Regius Pro-
fessor of Greek, Correspondence
edited by H. R. Luard. 1867
8vo Pub. No. viii
Porter, Jas., Shilling of James I. found
in Peterhouse Lodge Garden. 1884
R. xlv. ix

Portraits belonging to the University
before the Civil War C. iii. 275
Description of collection of
R. xliv. cxxix
Catalogue of the First Exhibition of
University and College Portraits,
held in the **Fitzwilliam Museum**,
May 1884, by J. W. Clark, 8vo.
3 Issues
Catalogue of the Second Exhibition
of University and College Portraits,
held in the Fitzwilliam Museum,
May 1885, by J. W. Clark, 8vo.
2 Issues
Portugal. See Mertola. *Alemquer*
Postumus, Coin C. v. 225
Pot, Earthenware, **found** in Great
St Mary's Passage R. xxxiii. 16
Pottery, Imitations R. xviii. 7
from Bethlehem, Burwell Fen, Cam-
bridge, Chesterford, Chesterton,
Cissbury, Cyprus, Downham Field,
Ditton, Ely, Foxton, Great Cotes,
Haddenham Fen, Haslingfield,
Loch Maree, Mildenhall, Nayland,
Ordsan, Steeple Morden, Swaff-
ham Fen, Trumpington, Wicken,
S. Utah: which see
See also Roman remains. Bottle.
Bust. Fibula. Jar. Kiln. Lamp.
Situla. Urn. Vase. &c.
Pottery-Rings from Switzerland
R. xlii. li
from Hauxton and Barrington
R. xlii. li
Powder-flask, xvi. century
R. xxxix. xix
Prague, Jews' Synagogue R. xii. 7
Prayer-book of K. Edward VI., at
Beccles C. i. 67
Preceptory at Shengay Pr. vii. 136
Preston, Suffolk, Brass, 1629, from
R. xli. xxii
Prideaux, Edmund, of Clare College
Pr. vii. 197
Primer, **Earliest** English, printed by
Wynkyn de Worde R. xxi. 9

Primer (*continued*)
  or Horae, Salisbury, 1474. Engrav-
    ings in Lambeth copy C. III. 257
Printers, Cambridge University, 1521—
    1884   C. v. 287
  See *Götz. Lettou. John Owen.*
  Plantin. John Siberch. Wynkyn
  de Worde
  Petition of Journeymen, *c.* 1611
                          R. xx. 7
Printing, Earliest example of, 1454
                        R. xxxvii. ix
  in New England, Establishment of
                        R. xxvi. 7
Prior, M., Unpublished Letters
              R. xiv. 7 : C. i. 99
Probus, Coins. See *Coins, Roman*
Prodigies recorded in history
                          R. viii. 4
Prussia. See *Cologne. Magdeburg.*
  Trier
Psalter, xv. century, written for John
  Harpur of Russhale
                      R. xxxviii. xvi
  in the University Library
                        Pr. viii. 146
  Greek, in Emmanuel College Library
                        Pr. viii. 168
Psammis, Fragment of Statue bearing
  the name   R. xlvi. lxiv
Ptolemaic manufacture, Oenochoe of
                        Pr. vii. 72
Purses, time of Charles I R. xxxvi. 15
Pyrenees, Pottery at Ordesan
              R. xxxvii. xii ; xl. xxvi
Pyrotechnie de Hanzelet Lorrain
                      R. xxxiii. 36
Pythagoras of Rhegion and the Coins
  of Selinus   R. xliv. cxxviii

Quarter Sessions Records, 1650—60,
  Bedfordshire   Pr. viii. 61
Quartzite Implements from Bois du
  Rocher, Ganterie, Dinan
                      R. xxxvi. 24
Queens' College. See *Cambridge*
Quy. See *Stow*

Radwell, Receipts for army taxes,
  1652—1658, for parsonage and
  glebe of   R. xxxiii. 19
Ram, Bronze, in Museum at Palermo
                      C. iii. 259
Rameses III., Sarcophagus of
                  C. iii. 371, 383
Raven, J. J., Church Bells of Cam-
  bridgeshire. Second edition, with
  a supplement and index. 1881—
  82   8vo Pub. Nos. xviii., xix
  Coins from Bartlow. 1880
                      R. xl. xx
  Roman bronze coins from Undley.
  1883   R. xliii. lxxvii
  Gnostic Signet. 1887
                  R. xlviii. cxxxiv
  Ravenna. Similarity of ornamental
    scrolls in the Mausoleum of Galla
    Placidia to sculptured stones in
    England   R. xliii. lxxviii
  Sculptured stones   R. xlvii. cxii
Reade, R. C., Minster-church at
  Aachen. 4 plates. 1882. C. v. 131
Recusants, Proclamation concerning
  Popish   R. xxvi. 7
Rede, Peter, Brass, with Flemish re-
  verse, xv. cent.   R. xii. 8
Rede, Sir Robert, by T. Brocklebank
                      C. i. 365
Redfern, W. B., xvi. century Powder-
  flask. 1879   R. xxxix. xix
  Italian Primer or Touch-box. 1879
                    R. xxxix. xix
  Early xvii. century wheel-lock
    Pistol. 1879   R. xxxix. xix
  xvii. century wheel-lock. 1879
                    R. xxxix. xix
  Unusually large horse-bell from
    Ireland. 1 plate. 1879.
                      R. xxxix. xix
  Bronze ring. 1879   R. xl. xii
  A tally-board. 1 plate. 1880
                    R. xl. xxviii
  English lamp and Roman pin dug
    up in Petty Cury. 1880
                    R. xli. xiii

Redfern, W. B. (*continued*)
Medieval Spurs. 1881 R. xli. xxiv
xv. century solleret "à la poulaine"
for the left foot. 1881
R. xli. xxv
Stirrups. 1881 R. xli. xxv
Horse-shoes dug up **near** Park-side.
1881 R. xli. xxv
Bottles in the collection of. 1892
Pr. viii. 60
Redmayne, R., MS. Life of Henry V.
R. xxi. 8
Registers, Parish. See *Parish*
Registry. See *Cambridge: University
Registry*
Reindeer, Engraving of **a** browsing,
from Thäingen. R. xxxvi. 10
Reliquary **from** Yorkshire
R. xlvii. cviii
from Rio Janeiro, Gold Pr. vii. 131
Reliquaries, Silver R. xxxvi. 21
Retables, Alabaster, from Milton and
Whittlesford Pr. vii. 106
Revesby Monastery, Catalogue **of**
Library R. xvi. 10: C. i. 97
Rhadegund, St.: see *St Radegund*
Rhadegund, St, Priory: **see** *Cam-
bridge*
Rhodes, W. A., Bronze medal, **dated
1794.** 1891 Pr. vii. 309
Rhodes, **Siege** of, Indulgence
R. xiii. 6
Rich, Sir **Nath., Letter** from Bp
Bedell C. ii. 95
Richardus Tertius, Dr Legge's tragedy
C. i. 347
Richmond and Derby, Margaret, Coun-
tess of. See *Beaufort*
Rickard, **J.** C., Four series of **Palæo-**
lithic **Implements from South**
Africa. **(6 plates.)** 1880
C. v. 57
**Neolithic Implements from South
Africa.** 1881 C. v. 67
Ridgeway, W., Roman bronze coins
from Ditton. 1883
R. xliii. lxxxvii

Ridgeway, W. (*continued*)
On Henry Middleton's paper on the
Legend of Atlantis. 1883
R. xliii. lxxxviii
Roman coins from Cottenham Fen.
1883 R. xliv. cvii
Ely token: "Wm. Gotobed, 1662."
1883 R. xliv. cvii
Are the Cambridgeshire ditches re-
ferred to by Tacitus? (1 plate.)
1891 Pr. vii. 200
Ridley, Gloucester. Account of Syriac
MS. of the New Testament
C. ii. 219
Rigg, John, **Letter of** the **time of**
James I. addressed by St. **John's**
College to the Countess of Shrews-
bury. 1852 C. i. 47
The orientation **of** King's College
Chapel. 1853 C. i. 59
Transcript of MS. references and
notes in Baker's copy of Newman's
Concordance. 1857 R. xvii. 10
Ring, *circa* 1450, with inscription
R. xii. 8
Brass finger, found in Cambridge
R. xliii. lxxxiii
Bronze, with head of **Jupiter**
R. xl. xii
Bronze, from Newton
Pr. vii. 185
found at Montpensier, supposed to
have belonged to the Black Prince
C. iv. 181
Signet. See *Signet*
Silver, xiv. century R. xxxvii. xiii
Ring-dial, Universal, 'Henry Sutton,
1660.' Pr. viii. 392
Ring-dials, from Abington Pigotts
Pr. vii. 130
from Cumberland
Pr. vii. 130
Ring-money, used by Liverpool mer-
chants on west coast of Africa
R. xli. xxv
from Wilburton Fen
R. xlv. xvii

Rings, Roman, from Chesterford
R. xlii. liv
Rio Janeiro, Gold Reliquary, etc.,
from Pr. vii. 131
Roads. See *British, Fen, Roman*
Robertson, J. D., Coining and the
implements of coining. (5 ill.)
1878 C. iv. 109
Robinson, Anne (of Gamlingay),
Confession, 1611 R. xviii. 7
Robinson, Matthew, MS. Autobio-
graphy R. xv. 9
Rockland, Chalice R. xli. xviii
Rogerson, Chas., Letter concerning
the christening of the Duke of
York R. xviii. 8
Rogerson, Robert, Letters testimonial
of the degree of M.A. granted to,
1653 R. xxv. 8
Rollestone Church, Herefordshire.
Sculptures R. x. 6
Roman antiquities found at Newton
Pr. vii. 185
buildings at Cirencester C. i. 55
camp (supposed) at Whitley, near
Alston C. vi. 41
causeway in Bridge Street, Cambridge R. xiii. 7
cemetery at Girton R. xli. xx
coins. See *Coins*
excavations at Fulbourn
C. iii. 313
graves at Hunstanton C. iv. 423
holding at Abington Pigotts
C. vi. 309
house at Swaffham Prior
Pr. viii. 173, 229
inscriptions. See *Inscriptions*
interments on Huntingdon Road
R. xxi. 8
interments by the Via Devana
C. ii. 289
medallions. "Stampare a conio."
How did the Romans stamp their
medallions? C. v. 33
monument at Turbia R. xxxviii. xiv
pottery. See *Pottery, Roman*

C. A. S. *Index.*

Roman (*continued*)
refuse pit in Alderney Pr. vii. 175
remains from Fen Ditton
R. xxxvi. 24
at Girton
R. xli. xxii; R. xlii. li
from Great Chesterford
R. xl. xvi; R. xlv. xii
from Haslingfield R. xxxvi. 25
from Newmarket R. xlv. xxi
from Rougham R. xli. xxii
from Shefford 4to Pub. No. x
from Shepreth R. xlvi. lx
from Wales R. xli. lx
from Wicken R. xl. xvi
See also *Bust. Fibula. Jar. Kiln.*
Lamp. Situla. Stone Implements.
Urn. Vase
Road, The Maiden Way C. vi. 41
from Cambridge to Godman-
chester R. xxi. 8
near Wicken R. xli. xvi
See also under *Fen*
Roads of Cambridgeshire R. x. 9 :
& 8vo Pub. Nos. iii. & xx
Roads. Via Appia R. xliv. cxxxv
Via Devana R. xliv. cxxxii
Signets found in the lead mines of
Charterhouse on Mendip
C. iv. 277
Station at Binchester R. xlii. xli
Villa at Comberton R. ix. 7
Villa at Hauxton R. xxxiii. 25
Wall in S. Germany R. xlii. xlvi
Romano-British Remains, by J. S.
Henslow 4to Pub. No. xii
Remains from Shefford
4to Pub. No. x.
Rome, Bonds not to procure dis-
pensations from R. xxxiii. 15
Sculptured stones R. xlvii. cxii
Rothley, Sculptured column
R. xlvi. lxxii
Rougham, Roman remains
R. xli. xxii
Royston, Lord, Medal commemorat-
ing his majority R. xxiii. 25

5

Royston, Gold Coins　　R. xlii. xxxvii
　Clock case　　　　　　R. viii. 5
　Notes on Limblow Hill　C. vi. 395
　Remains　　　　　R. xlviii. cxxxviii
Rubbish-pits, Roman　　　R. xli. xvi
Rud, Edward, sometime Fellow of
　Trinity College and R. of N.
　Runcton, Norfolk, Diary 1709—
　1720, edited by H. R. Luard.
　1860　　　　　　8vo Pub. No. v
Rule, Martin. Eadmer's elaboration
　of the first four books of the
　Historia Novorum in Anglia. (2
　plates.) 1886
　　　　　C. vi. 195; R. xlvi. lxvii
Church at Deerhurst. 1886
　　　　　　　　　R. xlvii. cii
Runic Calendar found in Lapland
　　　　　　　　　C. iv. 17
　Calendars, Four　　C. vi. 368
inscription on sculptured stone from
　Cheshire　　　　　Pr. vii. 86
Russhale, Staffs., John Harpur of,
　Psalter　　　　　R. xxxviii. xvi
Rutter, Arthur, Aureus of Nero from
　Pakefield, Suffolk. 1876
　　　　　　　　R. xxxvii. ix
Rye, Walter, Pedes Finium; or,
　Fines relating to the County of
　Cambridge, levied in the King's
　Court, from the vii. year of
　Richard I. to the end of the reign
　of Richard III. 1891
　　　　　　　8vo Pub. No. xxvi

Sabina, Empress, Coin　R. xliii. lxxxvi
Saffron Walden, Ancient Cemetery
　　　　　　　　R. xxxvi. 24
'Wool' weight, from Museum
　　　　　　　　R. xxv. 9
Saguntum, Keltiberian inscription
　　　　　　　　R. xli. xxiii
Sahidic dialect, Two fragments of Acts
　of Chamoul and Justus　C. i. 71
St Acheul, Flint Implements
　　　　　　　　R. xxxvi. 26

St Alban's Abbey, Glass in windows
　of the Library　　Pr. viii. 213
　Verses from Cloister windows
　　　　　　　　Pr. vii. 64
St Andrew, Legendary Adventures
　　　　　　　　R. ix. 5
　and St Veronica, Anglo-Saxon Le-
　gends, ed. by C. W. Goodwin,
　1851　　　　　8vo Pub. No. i
St Asaph, Remains found R. xxxix. xvi
St Catharine of Alexandria, Historical
　Enquiry touching, by C. Hard-
　wick. 1849　　4to Pub. No. xv
St Catharine's College. See Cambridge
St Cuthbert, Vestments R. xlvii. xciv
St Edmund's Abbey. See Bury St
　Edmunds
St Erasmus, Drawings of Martyrdom
　　　　　　　　R. xlvii. 102
　The Light of; and on the various
　spellings of his name　C. iv. 327
St George, Anglo-Saxon Notices
　　　　　　　　R. x. 10
St George of Cappadocia, Cultus
　　　　　　　　Pr. vii. 147
　Syriac and Coptic Versions of Mar-
　tyrdom　　　　Pr. vii. 133
St George and the Dragon, Frescoes
　　　　　　　　Pr. vii. 131
St John, Pawlet, Quatuor Orationes,
　1704　　　　　R. xxxiii. 36
St John's College. See Cambridge
St Lawrence, Seal　　R. xxxiii. 20
St Radegund, Lyfe of, circa 1520 C. i. 29
St Radegund's Priory. See Cambridge
St Veronica, Anglo-Saxon Legend of
　　　　　　　　C. i. 3
　and St Andrew. Anglo-Saxon Le-
　gends　　　　8vo Pub. No. i.
Sakit Canoes　　　　Pr. vii. 289
Salisbury Primer or Horae, 1494
　　　　　　　　C. iii. 237
Salle, John, Seal　　　C. vi. 345
Salmon, Peter, Letter to Samuel Col-
　lins, 1630　　　　C. iii. 211
Salonina, Empress, Coin　C. v. 225
Saloninus, Coin　　　　C. v. 225

Samian ware, Bowl   R. xlvii. cxii
    Dish   Pr. viii. 183
    Patera from Ely   R. xli. xxv
    Paterae   R. xxxiii. 31
    Two pieces of   R. xxxiii. 20
Sancroft, Archbishop. Form of prayer at consecration of Peterhouse Chapel   R. xxiv. 9
Sandars, S., Historical and Architectural Notes on Great St Mary's Church, Cambridge. Together with the Annals of the Church by E. Venables. (1 plate.) 1869   8vo Pub. No. x.
    Annotated list of books printed on vellum to be found in the Colleges and University of Cambridge. With an appendix containing a list of books referring to the bibliography of Cambridge Libraries. 1878   8vo Pub. No. xv.
Sandys, J. E., On an inscribed stone from Brough under Stanmore. 1885   R. xlv. xxix
    On H. F. Wilson's objects of interest from Trinity College. 1885   R. xlv. xxxi
Saracenic Arch at Garway   R. x. 6
Sarcophagus of Rameses III., Cover   C. iii. 371
    The Crook in the hand of Rameses III. on the cover   C. iii. 383
Sard. See Gem
Sault, Richard, mathematician   C. iii. 37
Sawston Cross   R. xliii. lxxvi
Sawston Hall, Chasubles   Pr. vii. 10
Sayer, Wm., tried for heresy, circa 1612   R. xxi. 8
Scala of Johannes Climacus Pr. vii. 17
Scarth, Henry John, Four antique gems. (4 ill.) 1877   R. xxxviii. iv, ix
School expenses, xvi. and xvii. centuries   C. v. 201
Scotland, Documents of Episcopal Church   C. ii. 225

Scotland (continued)
    Sculptured Stones. See Stones
    See St Asaph. Ceres. Fife. Flintshire. Mold
Scott, Christopher, Remarks on the Cultus of St George of Cappadocia. 1890   Pr. vii. 151
Scott, R. F., Letters of Sir Chris. Wren and N. Hawksmoor on a proposed New Bridge at St John's College, 1697–98. 1891   Pr. vii. 254
    Letters between St John's College and Trinity College, concerning the enclosure of Garret Hostel Green and Trinity College Walks, 1599—1600. 1891   Pr. vii. 261
Sculpture at Amiens Cathedral   R. xlviii. cxxxix
Sculptures in Rolleston Church, Herefordshire   R. x. 6
Scurgola, Spur   R. xli. xxv
Seal from Abergele   R. xxxix. xvi
    from Barnwell, of John the Baptist   R. xxxvi. 16
    of Wm. Cecil, Lord Burleigh   R. xix. 8
    of Sir Thos. Bysshe   R. xiii. 6
    of Prebend of Durham   R. xiii. 6
    of Galatius Episcopus Sarsinatensis   R. xvii. 9
    of Hospital of St John, Cambridge   R. xiii. 7
    of " S. Johannis ov Bois "   R. xxvi. 8
    representing St Lawrence, from Bottisham Fen   R. xxxiii. 20
    of Dudley, Earl of Leicester   R. xix. 8
    of Dean and Chapter of Lichfield   R. xxvi. 8
    of John Milton   R. xii. 8
    of Pilton Priory   R. ix. 8
    of John Salle   C. vi. 345
    of some Cambridge Priory   R. xxxvi. 21
Silver, temp. Charles II.   R. xxxiii. 31

Seals, Ancient, Impressions of
                        R. xix. 7
xvii. century   R. xxvi. 9
for bales   R. xxvi. 9
for labourers' passes
        R. x. 7; xvii. 10; C. i. 281
in wafer   R. xix. 8
King's, for passes, given to labourers
    and servants   C. i. 281
made out of Roman intaglios
                        R. x. 5
Medieval, and merchant's mark
                C. i. 5; iv. 187
Medieval   R. xi. 7; xxxiii. 27
of Edward III.   R. xi. 7
Searle, W. G., Coins, Tokens and
    Medals of the Town, County and
    University of Cambridge. 1871
        8vo Pub. No. xii.
History of Queens' College. Part i.
    1446—1560; Part ii. 1560—1662.
    1867—1871 8vo Pub. Nos. ix. xiii.
Ingulf and the Historia Croylanden-
    sis. An Investigation attempted.
    (1 plate.) 1894 8vo Pub. No. xxvii.
The Earliest Accounts and Inven-
    tories of Queens' College. 1857
                    R. xvii. 10
The Earliest Bursars' accounts of
    Queens' College. 1858
                    R. xviii. 9
Copper coin of Faustin, Empereur
    d'Haiti. 1860   R. xxi. 6
✓ Catalogue of the Library of Queens'
    College in 1472. 1862
            C. ii. 165; R. xxii. 7
Coin of Harthacnut from Oakington.
    1862   R. xxiii. 7
Some coins of Constantine the Great.
    1865   R. xxv. 10
List of Saxon coins struck at Cam-
    bridge. 1865   R. xxvi. 7
Dollar of Ferdinand, struck at
    Kempten, Bavaria, 1623. 1866
                    R. xxvi. 8
Penny of Henry II., King of Ger-
    many. 1866   R. xxvi. 8

Searle, W. G. (continued)
Books printed at Cambridge, 1521
    to 1700. 1867   R. xxxiii. 8
David Hood, print-seller at Cam-
    bridge, 1798. 1867 R. xxxiii. 8
Foreign and colonial coins, medals
    and tokens. 1868   R. xxxiii. 11
On the Liber Gratiarum A. 1868
                    R. xxxiii. 13
Cases of Chinese and Japanese Coins.
    1869   R. xxxiii. 16
List of Cambridge books and pam-
    phlets. 1869   R. xxxiii. 19
Medal in commemoration of Lord
    Royston's attaining his majority.
    1870   R. xxxiii. 25
Installation medal of Prince Albert.
    1871   R. xxxiii. 27
French and Eastern coins. 1872
                    R. xxxiii. 31
Exhibited a U.S. dollar of 1795,
    and a dollar note issued by the
    Confederate States. 1872
                    R. xxxiii. 35
French, Mexican, Japanese and other
    coins. 1872   R. xxxiii. 36
Various coins in his collection. 1873
                    R. xxxiii. 37
Palstaves found in the Fen near
    Ely. 1873   R. xxxvi. 9
Casts of ornaments on bells at Land-
    beach and Caldecote, Cambs., and
    Cold Ashby, Northants. 1873
                    R. xxxvi. 9
Flint implements from near Ely.
    1873   R. xxxvi. 9
Chinese coins and a Chinese Uni-
    versity medal. 1874 R. xxxvi. 11
Catalogue of Chinese coins. 1874
                    R. xxxvi. 11
Saxon beads from Foxton. 1876
                    R. xxxvi. 26
Origin and date of Ingulf's History
    of Croyland Abbey. 1890
                    Pr. vii. 207
Seaton, Bronze Fibula   R. xxxvi. 15
Sedan, Prisoner of. See Napoleon III.

Seebohm, F., Remarks on C. P. Teb-
butt's paper on Crooked Lands.
1885   R. xlvi. lxi
Selinus, Coin   R. xliv. cxxviii
Severina, Empress, Coin   C. v. 225
Severus, Coin   R. xliv. cvii
Shackle, Iron   R. xxxiii. 15
Shefford, Roman and Romano-British
Remains   4to Pub. No. x.
Coins   4to Pub. No. x.
Shelford, Great, Beads   R. xlvi. lx
Chantry   C. i. 214
Shelford, Little, Church: Result of an
excursion   R. viii. 6
Monuments in the Church
   4to Pub. No. xiv. Part 4
Shell implements from Barbadoes
   R. xxxvi. 22
Shells from Great Ormeshead
   R. xxxiii. 8
Shengay, Preceptory   Pr. vii. 136
Shepreth, Roman remains R. xlvi. lx
Chantry   C. i. 215
Sherlock, Thomas, Letter to Dr Ashton
 . C. ii. 195
Shetland, Antiquities of the immediate
past, from   Pr. viii. 314
Shields, British, from Coveney Fen
   R. vii. 4
from Isle of Ely
   4to Pub. No. xiv. Part 2
Shimield, W. H., On Shengay and its
Preceptory. 1890   Pr. vii. 136
Shoe, Elizabethan, Woodcut C. i. 51
Shrewsbury, Countess of, Letter from
St John's College   C. i. 47
Shuckburgh, E. S., Life of Dr Laurence
Chaderton. 1884 R. xliv. cxxix
Sibbes, Dr Richard, Materials for life
   C. i. 253
Siberch, John, Books printed at Cam-
bridge, 1521-2
   Pr. vii. 104; viii. 31
Letter from P. Kaetz to Pr. vii. 186
See R. Bowes's Biographical Notes
on the University Printers
   C. v. 283

Sicily. See Palermo
Sickle from Trumpington R. xl. xii
Sidney College. See Cambridge
Signet, Brass, with the head of St John
the Baptist in a charger
   R. xxxviii. xvi
British, from Stoney Hill, Laken-
heath   R. xlv. vii
Gnostic   R. xlviii. cxxxiv
Medieval British, from Lakenheath
   R. xlv. vii
of Eros   C. v. 363
Signet-ring of xv. century
   Pr. vii. 193
Silks in which St Cuthbert's body was
wrapped   R. xlvii. xcv
Sinai, Nawamees in the peninsula
   Pr. viii. 61
Sinker, R., Biographical Notes on the
Librarians of Trinity College. 1897
   8vo Pub. No. xxix.
Situla, Roman, from Great Chester-
ford   R. xxxiii. 24
Skeat, W. W., The Old English verbs
to lam and to lap. 1877
   R. xxxviii. xiii
Canoe found in the Ouse marshes.
1878   R. xxxix. xiii
Effigy of the bishop in Trinity
Church. 1879   R. xl. xiii
Remarks on discoveries at Barring-
ton. 1880   R. xli. xii
Remarks on the units of measure-
ment in Domesday. 1881
   R. xlii. xxxviii
Origin of the word garret. 1882
   R. xlii. xlix
On the word mirror. 1882
   R. xliii. lxxi
Remarks on G. F. Browne's paper
on Sculptured Stones in the N. of
England. 1882 R. xliii. lxxvi
Remarks on G. F. Browne's paper
on Sculptured Stones in Lothian.
1883   R. xliv. cxvi
Remarks on the study of Medieval
Glossaries. 1884 R. xliv. cxxvii

Skeat, W. W. (*continued*)
On the word *sol*. 1884   R. xlv. ix
A MS. leaf of a French metrical version of Guy of Warwick. 1887
  R. xlvii. cvii
Remarks on E. Magnússen's paper on Runic Calendars. 1888
  R. xlviii. cxxxvi
Etymology of the word *Amber*. 1893
  Pr. viii. 244
Skeleton, Part of human, from Burwell   R. xlvii. civ
Skeletons, Saxon, from Girton
  R. xlvi. lxxiv
Skull from Thetford   R. xlvii. xcvii
Skulls, Back of a large sized skull
  R. xxxiii. 31
Egyptian, Teeth of early
  R. xlvii. cx
Egyptian of the xxvi. dynasty
  Pr. vii. 17
from Harston   R. xlvii. cvii
from Steeple Morden   R. xl. xii
from Swaffham Fen   R. xliv. cxxix
Sletzstat, Device used by N. Gotz, printer of, 1474   C. iii. 237
Smith, A. H., Remarks on C. W. King's Etruscan Mirrors. 1882
  R. xliii. lxxii
Smith, G. C. Moore, On five MS. books by John Hall of Kipping. 1886
  R. xlvi. lxviii
Letters of John Gibson of St John's College, 1667-70. 1892
  Pr. viii. 64
A MS. Commonplace Book kept by John Duckworth of St John's College, about 1670. 1894
  Pr. viii. 333
Smith, J. J., Abbreviata Cronica ab Anno 1377 usque ad Annum 1469. (1 Facsimile.) 1840
  4to Pub. No. ii.
Specimens of College Plate. (13 plates.) 1845.   4to Pub. No. xi
Church Libraries : proposed paper
  R. vi. 12

Smith, J. J. (*continued*)
Extracts from letters on MSS. in College Libraries. 1848
  R. viii. 6
Result of an excursion to Little Shelford Church. 1848
  R. viii. 6
Church and Parochial Libraries. 1851   C. i. 33
MS. notes in a copy of K. Edward VI. First Prayer Book at Beccles. 1853   C. i. 67
Suggested sources for an Athenae Cantabrigienses. 1853   C. i. 65
Excavations of tumuli at Bincombe. 1854   C. i. 141
Key to Beloe's Sexagenarian. 1856
  R. xvi. 10
Smith, J. J., and E. Venables. Index to Baker MSS.
  R. ii. 4 ; iii. 5 ; iv. 5 ; vi. 4
'Smith' in A.-S. times   R. xlvii. xciv
Smyrna, Gem   R. xliv. cxxxv
Snuff-box, Dutch
  R. xxvi. 7 ; xxxvi. 20
Socket-celt, Bronze, from Willingham
  R. xxxvi. 10
'Sol,' On the word   R. xlv. ix
Solanus, Moses, M.A. by Royal Mandate, 1701.   C. v. 167
Solleret, xv. century   R. xli. xxv
Somersetshire. See *Halse*. *Mendip*
Spain. See *Saguntum*
Spanish Coins   R. xiii. 71
Spear-head, Bronze, from Walton on Thames   R. xl. xxii
Saxon, from Haslingfield
  R. xxxvi. 25
Spelman, Henry, Autograph, with some facts respecting him
  C. ii. 101
Spes Vetus, Statuette   C. iv. 67
Spindle-wheel from Haslingfield
  R. xxxvi. 23
Spoon from Wilburton   R. xlv. xvii
Spoon-bowl from Horningsey
  R. xlvi. lx

Spratt, Capt., Inscriptions in Crete.
R. xxiii. 8
Spur, Bronze, from Bottisham Lode
R. xxxvi. 13
Italian, from Scurgola, xvi. century
R. xli. xxv
xv. century R. xxxiii. 31
Spurs, Medieval R. xli. xxiv
from Newmarket R. xxxvi. 21
from Scurgola R. xli. xxv
Staffordshire. See Lichfield. Russhale
Stag, Red, Skeleton from Burwell Fen
R. xlv. xxx
Stag, Skeleton, from Manea Fen
Pr. vii. 2
Stag's Horn from Ditton R. xl. xxvii
from Stretham R. xlv. xvii
Stakes and pottery from a wattle-hut,
Loch Maree Pr. vii. 185
Stalls from Brampton Church, Hunts.
Pr. vii. 28
Stamford University Pr. vii. 2
"Stampare a conio." How did the
Romans strike their medallions?
C. v. 33
Stapleford, Sculptured columns
R. xlvi. lxxii
Stations of the Neolithic Age
R. xxxix. xvi
Statue of Athena Nikephoros
R. xli. xix
Statue bearing name Psammis
R. xlvi. lxiv
Statuette, Bronze, found near Earith,
Hunts. C. iii. 231
Egyptian bronze R. xxxvi. 23
from Grosseto R. xxxvi. 23
from near Royston
R. xlviii. cxxxviii
of Fortuna Nemesis C. v. 273
representing Spes Vetus C. iv. 67
Statuettes found at Tanagra
C. iii. 303
Stear, Henry (of Saffron Walden).
Stone implement and a terra-
cotta jug from Fen Ditton. 1881
R. xliv. cxxix

Steeple Morden, Pottery and skull
R. xl. xii
Stelae, Egyptian Pr. vii. 3; viii. 143
Stephens, George, Two fragments of a
MS. of Chaucer's Troilus and
Cresside. 1887 C. vi. 31
A vii. century leaf of the Lex Wisi-
gothica. 1887 C. vl. 337
Stevens, H. W. P., History of the
parish of Tadlow. 1890
Pr. vii. 189
Stewart, D. J., Transcript of a register
of some property belonging to the
monastery of Ely. 1871
R. xxxiii. 30
Stirrups R. xli. xxv
from Newmarket R. xxxvi. 21
Stoke, Suffolk, Frescoes R. ix. 8
Stokes, Henry, Newton's Schoolmaster
C. ii. 161
Stone, Cylindrical, from Barnwell
R. xxxiii. 13
Stone-grinder, from Vinovium
R. xli. xv
Stone-implements from St Acheul
R. xxxvi. 24
South Africa C. v. 57, 67
Amiens R. xxii. 6; xxiii. 8
Barbadoes R. xxxviii. xii
Barnwell C. iv. 177
Brittany R. xxxvi. 24
Cambridge R. xl. xiii
Canada R. xxxvi. 9
Canton R. xxxviii. xii
Cave of La Madelaine
R. xxxviii. xix
Chatteris R. xxxvi. 9
Chesterton gravel-pits R. xl. xiii
Cissbury R. xxxvi. 10
Cromer R. xxxvi. 21
Denmark R. xxxiii. 8, 20
Ditton R. xliv. cxxix
Ely R. xxxvi. 9
Grime's Graves R. xxxiii. 16, 26
Haslingfield
R. xxvi. 7; xxxvi. 25; xxxvii. xiii
Helwan, Cairo C. iv. 85

Stone-implements from (*continued*)
Horningsea   **R. xxxix. xi**
Islands of the Pacific
    R. xlviii. cxxxiv
Jutland   R. xxxvi. 16
Littleport   R. xli. xiv
Lough Glyn   R. xxxiii. 13
March   R. xlv. vii
Mildenhall   **R. xxxix. xi**
New England   **R. xxxviii. xii**
Newmarket   **R. xxxvi. 21**
Peru   **C. iv. 13**
Royston   R. xlviii. cxxxviii
Swaffham Fen   R. xxxiii. 15
Wales   R. xli. xvii
Spurious   **R. xvii. 10**
in Woodwardian Museum
    R. xxxviii. xii
Stone, Inscribed, of Scotland
    Pr. vii. 131
from Brough under Stanmore
    R. xlv. xxvii
Stone, Perforated, from Chesterton
    R. xxv. 9
from Ditton   R. xl. xxvii
Stones, Sculptured, at Ledsham
Church, Yorks.   R. xlvi. lxvii
Lincoln   R. xlv. xxx
Stapleford and Rothby, as bearing
on the dedication of places
    R. xlvi. lxxii
in British Museum, Guildhall &c.
    R. xliv. cxxxii
in Lothian, **Durham,** and Yorkshire
    R. xliv. cx
in North of England
    R. xliii. lxxiii
in Rome, **Ravenna,** Bologna and
Mantua   R. xlvii. cxii
presented by the Royal Architectural **Mus.**   R. xlvi. lvii
Similarity of ornamental scrolls **at**
Ravenna, to English
    R. xliii. lxxviii
with Ogham inscription Pr. vii. 88
with Runic inscription, from Che-
shire   Pr. vii. 86

Stones (*continued*)
On Inscriptions and **supposed In-**
scriptions   **C. vi. 1**
Stones discovered **in river bed at** Bar-
rington   **R. xliv. cxvi**
Stow-cum-Quy Chantry
    C. i. 201 : **R. xvi. 10**
Court Rolls   **R. xvii. 10**
Stowe, North, Hundred of : Seal for
labourers' passes   **R. xvii. 10**
Stowmarket, Medal from R. xxxiii. 13
Stradinger, Extracts from Annals of
Tewkesbury, relative to
    R. xxiii. 8
Stratford, Essex, Parish Registers
    R. xxvi. 7
Stretham, Stag's-horn, etc.
    R. xlv. xvii
Stuarts, Memorials of the
    R. **xlii. xxxvii**
Studiola at Pembroke College
    R. xxxix. xviii
at Caius College   **C. iii. 77**
Studs of belts from Iceland
    R. **xli. xxv**
Stuntney Fen, Horse-shoes
    R. xlvi. lxxi
Sturbridge Fair. See *Cambridge*
Suffolk. Survey of Manors in the
County   Pr. vi. 7
  See *Barnham.* **Beccles.** *Boxford.*
  Bury St Edmunds. Exning. Eye.
  Icklingham. Lakenheath. Milden-
  hall. Nayland. Pakefield. Pres-
  ton. Stoke. Stowmarket. Thurlow
Sulby Abbey, Northants., Bell
    R. xxxvi. 9
Sunday Observance in Charles II.'s
reign   **R. xxiii. 9**
Surrey. **See** *Thames.* **Walton on**
Thames
Sussex. See *Cissbury. Willingdon*
"Sutton, Henry, 1660," Universal
ring-dial   Pr. viii. 392
Swaffham, Norfolk, Catalogue of
library   **R. vi. 12**
Ditch near   **C. i. 95**

Swaffham, Norfolk (*continued*)
Chapman of, Legend
C. iii. 317; R. xliii. lxxxix
Swaffham Bulbeck, Excavations
Pr. vii. 221
Swaffham Fen, Coins, pottery and
celt R. xliv. cxxix
Stone implement R. xxxiii. 15
Swaffham Prior, Roman House
Pr. viii. 173, 229
Swainson, C. A. An Indulgence
printed in Germany, 1489. 1876
R. xxxvii. ix
Swavesey, Chantry C. i. 215
Switzerland. See *Avenches. Bienne.
Luzerne. Neuchatel*
Sword, Bronze, from near Ely
R. xlvii. xcviii
Iron, from Haslingfield
R. xxxvii. xiii
Swords, Eight C. iv. 377
Symbols, Sculptured stones, etc., in
Ledsham Church R. xlvi. lxvi
Synagogue at Prague R. xii. 7
Syracuse, Lamp R. xxxvi. 22
Syriac and Coptic versions of the
martyrdom of St George of Cappa-
docia Pr. vii. 133
Syriac MS. of the Pentateuch, Age
C. ii. 219
MS. of the New Testament, Glouces-
ter Ridley's account C. ii. 219

Tabula Peutingeriana C. v. 237
Tacitus, Cambridgeshire ditches re-
ferred to by Pr. vii. 200
Tacitus, Coin C. v. 225
Tadlow, History Pr. vii. 189
Takht-i-Bagh, Peshawur Valley, Grae-
co-Buddhistic fragments from
Pr. viii. 142
Tally-board and its use R. xl. xxviii
Tanagra, Statuettes from C. iii. 303
Tankard, Old Wooden C. iv. 219
Taylor, Chas. Exhibits portrait of
Alan Percy, Second Master of St
John's College. 1893 Pr. viii. 229

Taylor, Isaac. Remarks on T. McK.
Hughes' Excavations near New-
market. 1885 R. xlv. xxiii.
Remarks on an Inscribed Stone from
Brough under Stanmore. 1885
R. xlv. xxviii
Taylor, J. H. Exhibits a Pendant
Dial. 1890 Pr. vii. 135
Tebbutt, C. P. Existence and cause
of crooked lands. 1885
R. xlvi. lxi
Teeth of Egyptian skulls R. xlvii. cx
Temple of Apollo R. xlviii. cxxxvii
Tetricus, Coin of C. v. 225
Teversham, Bronze celt R. xxxvi. 11
Ornament R. xlviii. cxxxviii
Church, Wall-Paintings
R. xliii. lxii
Tewkesbury, Extracts from Annals
R. xxiii. 8
Thackeray, F. Cast of the seal of
Pilton Priory. 1849 R. ix. 8
Thüingen, Engraving of a browsing
reindeer from R. xxxvi. 10
Thames, Ivory knife-handle found in
the R. xxxvi. 21
Thebes, Inscribed block of clay
R. xlv. xxxix
Thetford, Skull and celt
R. xlvii. xcvii
Grimes Graves, near
R. xxxiii. 16; xxxvi. 26
Thomson, Hen. Collection of Graeco-
Buddhistic fragments found at
Takht-i-Bagh, in the Peshawur
Valley. 1892 Pr. viii. 148
Thornhill, Inscription R. xliv. cxxxiv
"Three Pigeons" Inn R. xliii. lxxi
Thurible from Elingheims Church in
the Island of Gothland R. xl. xiv
Thurlow, Great, Antiquities
Pr. vii. 252
Tincommius, Coin R. xl. xxvii
Tobacco-stopper from Burwell
R. ix. 7
Toft Monks, Brass in Church
R. xl. xxiv

Token found in Trinity Hall: 'Wm.
Limber,' Chesterton　R. xli. xii
from Ely (W. Gotobed, 1662)
　　　　　　　　　R. xliv. cvii
representing the Three Tuns
　　　　　　　　　R. xxxiii. 11
Tokens, Foreign　　R. xxxiii. 11
of the Town, County, and University
of Cambridge, by W. G. Searle.
1871　　　　　8vo Pub. No. xii
from Chesterton (15)
　　　　　　　　　R. xxxvi. 22
Tradesmen's, in Cambridgeshire,
during the latter part of the xvii.
century　　　　　C. i. 15
Touch-box, An Italian Primer or
　　　　　　　　　R. xxxix. xix
Touchstones from Cottenham
　　　　　　　　　R. xxxiii. xxvii
Tours, Celt　　　R. xxxviii. xix
Trajanus, Coins. See Coins, Roman
Treasure-trove, Law of　Pr. viii. 91
Trees, Age of　　R. xlii. xxxix, xlv
Treves. See Trier
Trier, Basilica and Porta Nigra
　　　　　　　　　R. xxxviii. xiii
Trinitarian House in Cambridge
　　　　　　　　　R. xxi. 8
Trinity College. See Cambridge
Trinity Hall.　See Cambridge
Triumph of Constantine　C. iv. 391
Trumpington, Cinerary urn
　　　　　　　　　R. xxxix. xvii
Sickle　　　　　R. xl. xii
Tudway, D. Reasons for the comple-
tion of his Degree in Music, a.d.
1705　　　　　　C. ii. 345
Tumuli, Formation of natural mounds
resembling　　　R. xxxvi. 26
near Bincombe, Dorsetshire
　　　　　　　　　C. i. 141
near Crosby Ravensworth
　　　　　　　　　R. xlv. xii
Upper Hare Park
　　　　　R. xxxvi. 26; xlv. ix
Tumulus near Newmarket
　　　　　　　　　R. xlv. xxii

Turbia, Monaco, Roman Monument at
　　　　　　　　　R. xxxviii. xiv
Tyery, Nicholas. Suggestions to
Henry VIII. for an Irish Coinage,
inserted in a MS. French Hand-
book, 1526. Edited by G. O.
White-Cooper and F. J. H. Jenkinson. 1886. (Illust. in text.)
　　　　　　　8vo Pub. No. xxii
Tympanum of the south door of Pampisford Church　　C. vi. 384
Tzetzes, Rare edition of, circa 1490—
1522　　　　　　R. xviii. 8

Uffenbach's Travels　R. xxii. 16
Unton, Sir Hen., Copies of corre-
spondence between Elizabeth and
Henry IV.　　　R. xxiv. 7
Upper Hare Park, Pottery
　　　　　　　　　R. xliv. cxxi
Tumuli　　R. xxxvi. 26; xlv. ix
Urns, Burial, found near the mouth
of the Amazon River　C. iv. 411
Cinerary　　　　R. xxxix. xviii
Cinerary from Nayland　R. xlvii. cv
Cinerary from Trumpington
　　　　　　　　　R. xxxix. xvii
Cinerary from St John's College and
Girton　　　　　Pr. viii. 282
Cinerary from Peru　R. xl. xxvii
Romano-British, from near the
Observatory　　　R. xxxix. xi
Utah, South, Pre-historic pottery
　　　　　　　　　R. xliv. cvii
Utrecht Breviary, 1514. Engravings
fastened in Cambridge copy
　　　　　　　　　C. iii. 255

Valens, Coin　　　R. xliii. lxxvii
Valentinianus, Coin　R. xl. xvii
Vase, British, from Ditton
　　　　　　　　　R. xxxvii. xii
from near Chesterford
　　　　　　　　　R. xxxvii. xiii
Glass, from Anstey　R. xxxviii. xviii
Inscribed, from Guilden Morden
　　　　　　　　　C. iv. 337

Vase (continued)
Mantuan. See Mantuan
Roman, from Huntingdon Road
R. xxxiii. 13
Romano-British, from Chesterton
Road R. xxxiii. 11
from Coldham Common
R. xxxviii. xi
from Ely R. xli. xxv
from Haddenham Fen R. xl. xii
from Hunstanton C. iv. 423
Silver-gilt, xv. century
R. xlii, xxxvi
Terra-cotta, from Downham Field
R. xlii. xlvii
from West Row Fen R. xliii. lxxi
from Upper Hare Park
R. xliv. cxxi
Vases, British, from Mepal Fen
R. xx. 7
from Bethlehem Hospital
R. xxxvi. 11
from Coldham Common
R. xxxiii. 11
from King Street R. xlii. 1
in Cemetery at Steeple Morden
R. xl. xii
Roman, found near Cambridge
R. xxxiii. 20
Vellum, Books printed on. See Books
Venables, Edm., Annals of the Church
of Great St Mary's, Cambridge.
1869. 8vo Pub. No. x
The Nonae Rolls, as they relate to
Cambridgeshire. 1850 C. i. 7
Extracts from the Essex MSS. in the
British Museum. 1856 R. xvi. 10
Sculptured stone discovered at Lin-
coln. 1885 R. xlv. xxx
Formation of the Diocese of Ely.
1890 Pr. vii. 157
and J. J. Smith. Index to Baker
MSS. R. ii. 4; iii. 5; iv. 5; vi. 4
Venn, J. Register of Baptisms, Mar-
riages and Burials in St Michael's
Parish, Cambridge, 1538—1837.
1891 8vo Pub. No. xxv

Ventris, E., Costume in the Univer-
sity. 1849 R. ix. 8
Statement in Lysons' Cambridge-
shire concerning Malketon. 1851
R. xii. 7
The third Esquire Bedell, 1556.
1853 R. xiii. 7
Silver Coin of Henry VI. 1853
R. xiii. 8
Chantries and Free Chapels; with
some account of those in the
County of Cambridge; together
with the foundation charter of
Anstey's chantry at Stow-cum-Quy.
(Illustration of Brass of John An-
stey, at p. 219.) 1856 C. i. 201
Foundation deed of the Anstey
Chantry in Quy Church and the
brass attributed to Dengain. 1856
R. xvi. 10
The British Merlin for 1751. 1857
R. xvii. 10
Extracts from Court Rolls of Stow-
cum-Quy. 1857 R. xvii. 10
Documents relating to the case of
Wm. Sayer in the Consistory
Court of John Jegon, Bp of
Norwich, c. 1612. 1861 R. xxi. 8
MS. list of English contributions to
the Convent of English Francis-
cans at Douay, 1630—1649.
1861 R. xxi. 9
Church Music in Ashwell Church.
1862 R. xxii. 7
Churchwardens' accounts at Bass-
ingbourne. 1862 R. xxii. 7
Attempts made in the reign of
Charles II. to pass an Act of
Parliament for the better obser-
vance of the Lord's Day. 1863
R. xxiii. 9
Certain lapsed legacies by Dr James
Johnson to Sidney College in
1688. 1863 R. xxiii. 9
Iron knife found in making the
bridge between Horningsey and
Waterbeach. 1874 R. xxxiv. 10

Verica, Coin   R. xl. xxvii.
Veronica, St, Anglo-Saxon legend of
    O. i. 3
    and St Andrew, Anglo-Saxon legends
    8vo Pub. No. 1
Vespasianus, Coin   R. xxxiii. xxvii
Vessel, Bronze ornament on, from
    Farndale   R. xxxiii. 30
    Earthen, from Comberton   R. ix. 7
    Earthenware, from Haslingfield
       R. xxxix. xii
    Leaden, from Willingdon
       R. xxxix. xviii
    Leaden, from Westley Waterless
       R. xxxix. xiv
    Leaden, from Trinity College Library
       R. xxxix. xiv
Vessels, Terra-cotta, from Cyprus
       R. xl. xx
    Sepulchral, from Warden, Materials
    of   4to Pub. No. xii
Vestments of St Cuthbert
       R. xlvii. xciv
    in Churchwardens' books of Bassing-
    bourne   R. xxxiii. 11, 13
Veysy family, House of, Cambridge
       Pr. vii. 93
Via Appia, Stones   R. xliv. cxxxv
Via Devana, On the   R. xliv. cxxxii
    Roman interments   C. ii. 289
Victoria, Queen, Gold pattern Crown
    piece   R. xxxvi. 15
Victorinus, Coin   C. v. 225
Victuallers' Licenses, 1653-4   R. xxi. 7
Vigani, John Francis, first Professor
    of Chemistry   Pr. viii. 380
Vinovium, co. Durham, Stone grinder
       R. xli. xv
Visceral or so-called Canopic Jar
       R. xliv. cxxxi
Visitation of the Archdeaconry of Ely,
    1685   C. iii. 323
    of the Churches of Pelham Fur-
    neaux and Brent Pelham, Herts.,
    1297   C. iii. 53
    of the County of Cambridge, Heralds'
       C. ii. 67

Volcanoes of Central France, Activity
    of   R. xxv. 7
Vows of Widowhood in the xiv. xv.
    and xvi. centuries   C. i. 71

Wace, F. C. Rubbing of an inscrip-
    tion on a mural tablet on a corn-
    mill, near Fountains Abbey. 1870
       R. xxxiii. 20
    Glass bottle, probably Phoenician.
    1875   R. xxxvi. 15
    Rubbing of an incised slab in the
    Dutch language, in St Mary's
    Church, Haddiscoe. 1880
       R. xl. xxiv
    Brass in Toft Monks Church. 1880
       R. xl. xxiv
    Copper ornament from Teversham.
    1888   R. xlviii. cxxxviii
    Exhibited the Will of General Bene-
    dict Arnold, 1781. 1889
       Pr. vii. 18
Waldensian Manuscripts, Recovery of
    the long lost   C. ii. 203
Wahlstein, C. Resemblances between
    the works of different races.
    1883   R. xliii. cxxxviii
    Pythagoras of Rhegion and the coins
    of Selinus. 1884
       R. xliv. cxxviii
    Macedonian coins as illustrating the
    gradual degeneracy of athletic
    games. 1884   R. xliv. cxxviii
    Stones from the Via Appia, in the
    Fitzwilliam Museum. 1884
       R. xliv. cxxxv
    Red jasper intaglio from Smyrna.
    (1 illust. in text.) 1884
       R. xliv. cxxxv
Wales, Ancient tribes of North
       R. xli. xvii
    Felstone implements from the valley
    of the Elwy   R. xli. xvii
    Hill-forts of North   R. xli. xvii
    Roman remains   R. xli. xi
    See Abergele. Castell. Great Ormes-
    head. Lleithvaen

Walker, Bryan. Discoveries made during the recent restoration of Landbeach Church. 1879. (2 plates and 4 ill.) C. IV. 245

Measurements and valuations of the Domesday of Cambridgeshire. 1881 R. XLII. xxxix; C. v. 93 and Atlas of 'Tables' in folio

Terrier of Landbeach, drawn up in 1549 by Archb. Parker. 1882 R. XLII. lxxx

The Tabula Peutingeriana. 1883. (2 maps in text.) C. v. 237

Remarks on O. C. Pell's paper on Libere tenentes, etc., and the word wara. 1884 R. XLV. viii

The Inquisitio Comitatus Cantabrigiensis. 1884 C. VI. 45. Discussion R. XLV. ix

Remarks on land measurements in Domesday. 1884 R. XLV. xi

Ancient Camps in Wiltshire and adjoining counties, and on non-military Camps. 1884 R. XLV. xiv; XLVI. lxxi

Remarks on O. C. Pell's paper on Domesday Geldable Hide. 1885 R. XLV. xvii

Walker, F. A., Specimens of S. American pottery. 1880 R. XL. xx

Walker, J., Axes, probably Saxon, from Newmarket Heath. 1876 R. XXXVI. 21

Spur, Stirrup, and Lance-head from Newmarket Heath. 1876 R. XXXVI. 21

Walton on Thames, Bronze Spearhead R. XL. xxii

'Wara,' On the word R. XLV. viii

Waraker, Thos., Letter on the Law of Treasure Trove. 1892 Pr. VIII. 91

Warbeck, Perkin, Coin R. XL. xx

Warden, Beds., Two vessels found at, by J. S. Henslow 4to Pub. No. XII

Warren, Rich., Letter to Dr Ashton C. II. 195

'Warren's Book,' Trinity Hall R. XL. xxi

Waterbeach Church, Glass R. XXXIII. 27

Coin R. XXII. 6

History, by W. K. Clay, 1859 8vo Pub. No. XIV

Wat's Dyke, Flintshire R. XLI. xiii

Wattle-Hut, Loch Maree, Stakes and pottery Pr. VII. 185

Way, Albert, Seals used to authenticate the passes of labourers. 1850 R. X. 7

Some medieval seals in the collection of the Society. 1850 C. I. 5; R. XI. 7

Mortuary Roll sent forth by the Prior and Convent of Ely, on the death of John de Hotham, Bishop of Ely, deceased Jan. 1336–7. 1854 C. I. 125; R. XXVI. 8

King's seals for passes given to labourers and servants, in accordance with the statute passed at the parliament of Cambridge, Sept. 12. Ric. II. A.D. 1388. (Illustrations in text.) 1857 C. I. 281

Weapons. See Stone Implements

Wedge of bronze from Arkesden R. XXXVI. 15

Weight, A flat brass R. XXXIX. xix

Well, Ancient, at Mount Sorrel Pr. VIII. 133

Wells Cathedral, Chained library Pr. VIII. 1

Welsh Language, The oldest written remains of C. III. 263

Wenman, Agnes Lady, translator of Zonaras C. II. 327

West Indian Islands, Charab Implements C. III. 295

Westley Waterless, Leaden vessel R. XXXIX. xiv

Paten from R. IX. 21

West Mere, Wretham, Norfolk C. I. 339

Westminster Abbey, Tomb of the
Countess of Richmond and Derby
C. v. 265

Westmoreland. See *Crosby. Ravensworth*

Weston Colville, Brass in Church,
circa 1430   R. xl. xii

West Row Fen, Mildenhall, Vase and
Roman Coins   R. xliii. lxxi

Whaddon Chase, Coin   R. xxxiii. 35

Wheel-lock, xvii. century
R. xxxix. xix

Whewell, Wm., Death. 1866 R. xxvi. 8

White, W., Roman kiln at Great Chee-
terford. 1880. (1 plate.)
R. xl. xxvii

Roman graves at Hunstanton. 1880.
(1 plate.)   C. iv. 423

So-called rubbish pits commonly
found associated with Roman remains. 1880   R. xli. xvi

"Moats" at Caxton. 1883
R. xliii. lxxxiii

Roman Horse-shoe from Caxton.
1883   R. xliii. lxxxiii

Finger-ring dug up at Cambridge.
1883   R. xliii. lxxxiii

Part of a Roman Millstone from
Great Eversden. 1883
R. xliii. lxxxiii

Squeeze of a stone with a cuneiform
inscription, from Nineveh. 1883
R. xliii. lxxxiii

Objects of antiquarian interest dug
up in Trinity College. 1893.
(1 ill.)   Pr. viii. 292

White-Cooper, G. O., and F. J. H.
Jenkinson. N. Tyery's Irish Coinage. 1886   8vo Pub. No. xxii

Whitehall, Rob., Bible Prints, 1677
R. xxxvii. xii

Whitehouse, F. C., The Lake of Moeris and the patriarch Joseph.
1885   C. vi. 177

Whitley, near Alston, Northumberland, Supposed Roman Camp
C. vi. 41

Whittlesford, Alabaster retable
Pr. vii. 106

Whitwick, **Monastery**
R. xlviii. cxxxvii

Wicken, Roman remains   R. xli. xv

Widdrington, Ralf, Answer to his **Pe**-
tition   R. xix. 8

Wilbraham, Amber necklace
R. viii. 6

Wilbraham Parva, Deeds, 1439—1646
R. xlviii. cxxxviii

Chantry   C. i. 216

Wilburton, Horn   R. xlv. xvii

Gold Ring-money   R. xlv. xvii

Silver Spoon   R. xlv. xvii

Wilkinson, C. A., Silver-gilt vase of
xv. **century.** 1881 R. xlii. xxxvi

Will of General Arnold   Pr. vii. 18

Sir John Hampden, 1457
R. xix. 8

Dr Thos. Lane   R. xx. 7

William and Mary, Coin R. xxxvi. 15

Williams, Archbishop, Letters and
materials for life
C. ii. 25; iii. 61

Williams, A. H., **Glass Beads, an iron
blade, and fibulae** from Landesborough Park. 1884
R. xliv. cxxix

Williams, Geo., Notices of W. Millington, first provost of King's College. 1858   C. i. 287

Documents from the Rolls Office
concerning Bp John **Langton.**
1858   R. xix. 7

**Manumissions of Serfs extracted
from the records of King's Col-**
lege. 1859   C. i. 359; R. xix. 7

Seal of the Dean and Chapter of
Lichfield. 1865   R. xxvi. 8

Seal inscribed 'S. Johannis ov Bois.'
1865   R. xxvi. 8

Williams, Walter (of Broomy-Hill),
Dutch Snuff-box. 1875
R. xxxvi. 20

Willingdon, Sussex, Leaden vessel
R. xxxix. xviii

Willingham, Bronze socket-celt
  R. xxxvi. 10
  Chantry C. i. 216
  Key R. xxxiii. 8
  Roman coins C. v. 225
Willis, R., Description of the Sextry
  Barn at Ely, lately demolished.
  (4 plates.) 1843 4to Pub. No. vii.
  Architectural Nomenclature of the
  Middle Ages. (3 plates.) 1844
  4to Pub. No. ix
  Arrangement of monastic buildings.
  1847 R. vii. 3
  Case of a clock from near Royston.
  1847 R. viii. 5
  Pavement in Canterbury Cathedral.
  1848 R. ix. 7
  Saracenic Arches. 1848 R. x. 6
  Discoveries in the choir of Lichfield
  Cathedral. 1860 R. xxi. 6
  Death. 1875 R. xxxvi. 17
Willoughby, Richard, Arms
  Pr. viii. 337
Wills of Eminent Persons, Remarks
  on a recently published selection
  C. ii. 337
Wills at King's College, Cambridge
  R. xx. 8
Wilson, H. F., Inscription in Ashwell
  Church, Hertfordshire, respecting
  the Black Death. 1885 R. xlv. xvi
  Rubbing of incised picture on wall
  of Ashwell Church. 1885
  R. xlv. xvii
  Objects of interest discovered in an
  attic in Trinity College. 1885
  R. xlv. xxxi
  The Brandon flint-trade. 1885
  R. xlv. xxxiii
Wilton family. School and College
  Expenses, xvi. and xvii. cents.
  C. v. 201
Wiltshire, Camps
  R. xlv. xiv ; xlvi. lxxi
Wimpole, Chantry C. i. 216
Winchester Cathedral, Paintings
  Pr. viii. 100

Winwick, Cross R. xlvii. cvi
Witt, Samuel, Two upper mill-stones
  from Lakenheath. 1880 R. xl. xx
  Horns of Bos Primigenius. 1885
  R. xl. xx
Wood, E. G. de S., The University of
  Stamford. 1888 Pr. vii. 2
  Remarks on J. H. Middleton's Altar-
  Cloth from Lyng Church. 1888
  Pr. vii. 7
  Note on the cultus of St George of
  Cappadocia. 1890 Pr. vii. 147
  Formation of the ancient Diocese of
  Ely. 1890 Pr. vii. 157
  Remarks on E. G. Duff's paper on
  a recently discovered fragment of
  an unknown book printed by John
  Lettou. 1890 Pr. vii. 192
Woodham, H. A., Application of He-
  raldry to the illustration of va-
  rious University and Collegiate
  Antiquities. (Plates.) 1841-2
  4to Pub. Nos. iv. and v.
Woodlark, Robert, founder and first
  master of St Catharine's Hall
  C. i. 329
  Petition for foundation charter for
  St Catharine's Hall R. ii. 4
'Wool' weight from Saffron Walden
  R. xxv. 9
Words, List of most uncommon
  C. iv. 310
  See Latin
Worked Flints. See Stone Implements
Wortham, B. H., Churchwardens' Ac-
  counts of Bassingbourn. 1880
  R. xl. xxii
Wren, Sir C., Letter to St John's
  College, on proposed new bridge
  Pr. vii. 254
Wretham, near Thetford, West Mere
  C. i. 339
Wright, A. G., Leaf-shaped arrow-
  head from Newmarket. 1881
  R. xlii. xlii
  Naturally-formed celt from Ickling-
  ham. 1881 R. xlii. xlii

Wright, A. G. (*continued*)
 Terra-cotta head in high relief from
  Icklingham. 1882 R. XLIII. lxxii
 Bone dagger **from** Burwell Fen.
  1882 R. XLIII. lxxii
 Bronze fibula from Diss. 1883
  R. XLIII. lxxxvi
 Roman coins from Exning. 1883
  R. XLIII. lxxxv
 British terra-cotta vase from Upper
  Hare Park. 1884 **R.** XLIV. cxxi
 Roman coins and part of a terra-
  cotta handle from Newmarket.
  1884 R. XLIV. cxxi
 Celt, part of a skull and Roman
  pottery from Swaffham Fen. 1884
  R. XLIV. cxxix
 Five billon **denarii** of Posthumus.
  1884 R. XLV. vii
 Roman ear-ring and medieval signet-
  ring from Lakenheath. 1884.
  R. XLV. vii
 Photograph of stone implement from
  New Park. 1884 R. XLV. vii
 Antiquities found near Newmarket
  and presented **to** the Society.
  1891 Pr. VII. 307
 Exhibited gold coin found in plough-
  ing near Great Malvern. 1890
  Pr. VII. 135
Wright, W. Aldis, Entries relating to
 the marriage and children of John
 More, apparently **the** father of Sir
 Thomas More. 1868 C. III. 199

Wright, W. Aldis (*continued*)
 Election of **Sir Francis** Bacon and
  Dr Barnaby **Goche** as Burgesses
  in Parliament, April 1614, written
  by Dr Duport. 1868 C. III. 203
 'Wright' in Anglo-Saxon times
  R. XLVII. xciv
Wynkyn de Worde, Salisbury Primer
 or Horae, 1494, printed by
  R. XXI. 9 ; C. III. 257
 Book printed by, 1502
  R. XLVII. cii
Wyvern, Crystal bowl representing
  Pr. VIII. 390

York, Duke of [James II.]. Letter
 concerning his Christening, 1639
  R. XVIII. 8
York Cathedral, Parallelism in Lich-
 field Cathedral and **R. XXI. 7**
 West towers **C. III. 269**
York, Intaglio Medallion **found at**
  R. XXXVI. 25
Yorkshire, **Dialect** of North **R.** VIII. 5
 Reliquary R. XLVII. cviii
 Sculptured **stones** R. XLIV. cx
 See also *Bilton. Catterick. Croft.
 Farndale. Kirkby Wharfe. Led-
 sham. Pickering. Thornhill*

Zonaras, Agnes Lady Wenman, **the**
 translator of C. II. 327
Zutphen, Chained Library
  R. XLVI. lxix ; Pr. VIII. 359

www.ingramcontent.com/pod-product-compliance
Lightning Source LLC
Chambersburg PA
CBHW032357280326
41935CB00008B/603